DEFENSE, SECURITY AND STRATEGIES

U.S. SPECIAL OPERATIONS FORCES: POLICIES, FUNCTIONS AND DOCTRINES

DEFENSE, SECURITY AND STRATEGIES

Additional books in this series can be found on Nova's website
under the Series tab.

Additional E-books in this series can be found on Nova's website
under the E-books tab.

AMERICAN POLITICAL, ECONOMIC, AND SECURITY ISSUES

Additional books in this series can be found on Nova's website
under the Series tab.

Additional E-books in this series can be found on Nova's website
under the E-books tab.

DEFENSE, SECURITY AND STRATEGIES

U.S. SPECIAL OPERATIONS FORCES: POLICIES, FUNCTIONS AND DOCTRINES

MICHAEL E. HARRIS
AND
ROGER L. COOK
EDITORS

Nova Science Publishers, Inc.
New York

Copyright © 2011 by Nova Science Publishers, Inc.

All rights reserved. No part of this book may be reproduced, stored in a retrieval system or transmitted in any form or by any means: electronic, electrostatic, magnetic, tape, mechanical photocopying, recording or otherwise without the written permission of the Publisher.

For permission to use material from this book please contact us:
Telephone 631-231-7269; Fax 631-231-8175
Web Site: http://www.novapublishers.com

NOTICE TO THE READER

The Publisher has taken reasonable care in the preparation of this book, but makes no expressed or implied warranty of any kind and assumes no responsibility for any errors or omissions. No liability is assumed for incidental or consequential damages in connection with or arising out of information contained in this book. The Publisher shall not be liable for any special, consequential, or exemplary damages resulting, in whole or in part, from the readers' use of, or reliance upon, this material. Any parts of this book based on government reports are so indicated and copyright is claimed for those parts to the extent applicable to compilations of such works.

Independent verification should be sought for any data, advice or recommendations contained in this book. In addition, no responsibility is assumed by the publisher for any injury and/or damage to persons or property arising from any methods, products, instructions, ideas or otherwise contained in this publication.

This publication is designed to provide accurate and authoritative information with regard to the subject matter covered herein. It is sold with the clear understanding that the Publisher is not engaged in rendering legal or any other professional services. If legal or any other expert assistance is required, the services of a competent person should be sought. FROM A DECLARATION OF PARTICIPANTS JOINTLY ADOPTED BY A COMMITTEE OF THE AMERICAN BAR ASSOCIATION AND A COMMITTEE OF PUBLISHERS.

Additional color graphics may be available in the e-book version of this book.

Library of Congress Cataloging-in-Publication Data

Harris, Michael E.
  U.S. Special Operations Forces : policies, functions and doctrines / Michael E. Harris and Roger L. Cook.
    p. cm.
  Includes index.
  ISBN 978-1-61470-507-9 (hbk.)
  1. Special forces (Military science)--United States. 2. U.S. Special Operations Command. 3. Special operations (Military science)--United States. I. Cook, Roger L. II. Title.
  UA34.S64.H38 2011
  356'.160973--dc23
                    2011024677

Published by Nova Science Publishers, Inc. † New York

CONTENTS

Preface		**vii**
Chapter 1	U.S. Special Operations Forces (SOF): Background and Issues for Congress *Andrew Feickert and Thomas K. Livingston*	**1**
Chapter 2	USSOCOM Fact Book *Special Operations Forces*	**13**
Chapter 3	Special Operations *Joint Publication 3-05*	**53**
Chapter 4	Posture Statement of Admiral Eric T. Olson, USN Commander, United States Special Operations Command, before the 112th Congress, House Armed Services Committee *Eric T. Olson*	**127**
Chapter Sources		**135**
Index		**137**

PREFACE

Special Operations Forces (SOF) are elite military units with special training and equipment that can infiltrate into hostile territory through land, sea or air to conduct a variety of operations, many of them classified. SOF personnel undergo rigorous selection and lengthy specialized training. The U.S. Special Operations Command (USSOCOM) oversees the training, doctrine and equipping of all U.S. SOF units. This book examines the background and issues for Congress of the U.S. Special Operations Forces with a focus on their history, mission and priorities, as well as their core activities.

Chapter 1- Special Operations Forces (SOF) play a significant role in U.S. military operations, and the Administration has given U.S. SOF greater responsibility for planning and conducting worldwide counterterrorism operations. U.S. Special Operations Command (USSOCOM) has close to 60,000 active duty, National Guard, and reserve personnel from all four services and Department of Defense (DOD) civilians assigned to its headquarters, its four components, and one sub-unified command. The 2010 Quadrennial Defense Review (QDR) directs increases in SOF force structure, particularly in terms of increasing enabling units and rotary and fixed-wing SOF aviation assets and units. USSOCOM Commander, Admiral Eric T. Olson, in commenting on the current state of the forces under his command, noted that since September 11, 2001, USSOCOM manpower has nearly doubled, the budget nearly tripled, and overseas deployments have quadrupled; because of this high level of demand, the admiral added, SOF is beginning to show some "fraying around the edges" and one potential way to combat this is by finding ways to get SOF "more time at home." Admiral Olson also noted the effectiveness of Section 1208 authority, which provides funds for SOF to train and equip regular and irregular indigenous forces to conduct counterterrorism operations.

Chapter 2- Two aircrafts crashed. Eight servicemembers lost their lives. Fifty-three hostages remained in captivity. Operation Eagle Claw was a heroic effort, but this tragic secret mission in April 1980 showed the need for a joint Special Operations Force, leading to the creation of U.S. Special Operations Command.

The operation occurred at a remote site in Iran known as Desert One, and its purpose was to rescue 53 American hostages held at the U.S. Embassy in Tehran, Iran. Servicemembers from the Army, Navy, Air Force and Marine Corps were involved in the operation, but miscommunication, lack of standardized training among the branches and other external factors caused the mission failure, which showed the need for a unified, multi-service Special Operations command.

Chapter 3- Special operations (SO) differ from conventional operations in degree of physical and political risk, operational techniques, modes of employment, and dependence on detailed operational intelligence and indigenous assets. SO are conducted in all environments, but are particularly well suited for denied and politically sensitive environments. SO can be tailored to achieve not only military objectives through application of special operations forces (SOF) capabilities for which there are no broad conventional force requirements, but also to support the application of the diplomatic, informational, and economic instruments of national power.

Chapter 4- My intent today is to describe the current status, activities and requirements of Special Operations Forces. I'll begin by briefly describing USSOCOM and its assigned Special Operations Forces.

As many of you know, USSOCOM is a creation of Congress, legislated into being in 1986. A relatively small number of Army, Navy and Air Forces units designated as Special Operations Forces were assigned to USSOCOM, with Marine Corps forces joining the Command just over five years ago.

In: U.S. Special Operations Forces
Editor: Michael E. Harris and Roger L. Cook

ISBN: 978-1-61470-507-9
© 2011 Nova Science Publishers, Inc.

Chapter 1

U.S. SPECIAL OPERATIONS FORCES (SOF): BACKGROUND AND ISSUES FOR CONGRESS

Andrew Feickert and Thomas K. Livingston

SUMMARY

Special Operations Forces (SOF) play a significant role in U.S. military operations, and the Administration has given U.S. SOF greater responsibility for planning and conducting worldwide counterterrorism operations. U.S. Special Operations Command (USSOCOM) has close to 60,000 active duty, National Guard, and reserve personnel from all four services and Department of Defense (DOD) civilians assigned to its headquarters, its four components, and one sub-unified command. The 2010 Quadrennial Defense Review (QDR) directs increases in SOF force structure, particularly in terms of increasing enabling units and rotary and fixed-wing SOF aviation assets and units. USSOCOM Commander, Admiral Eric T. Olson, in commenting on the current state of the forces under his command, noted that since September 11, 2001, USSOCOM manpower has nearly doubled, the budget nearly tripled, and overseas deployments have quadrupled; because of this high level of demand, the admiral added, SOF is beginning to show some "fraying around the edges" and one potential way to combat this is by finding ways to get SOF "more time at home." Admiral Olson also noted the effectiveness of Section 1208 authority, which provides funds for SOF to train and equip regular and irregular indigenous forces to conduct counterterrorism operations.

Vice Admiral William McRaven, the current commander of the Joint Special operations Command (JSOC) has been recommended by the Secretary of Defense for nomination to replace Admiral Olson, who is retiring this year, as USSOCOM Commander. USSOCOM's FY2012 Budget Request is $10.5 billion—with $7.2 billion in the baseline budget and $3.3 billion in the Overseas Contingency Operations (OCO) budget, representing an increase of seven percent over the FY2011 Budget Request of $9.8 billion.

There are potential issues for congressional consideration. U.S. SOF in Iraq are in the process of transitioning counterterror operations in Iraq to Iraqi SOF and lessons learned could assist Congress in its oversight role. Another issue is that on January 6, 2011, Secretary of Defense Gates and Chairman of the Joint Chiefs of Staff Admiral Mike Mullen announced starting in FY2015, the Army would decrease its permanently authorized endstrength by 27,000 soldiers and that the Marines would lose anywhere between 15,000 to 20,000 Marines. Because USSOCOM draws their operators and support troops from the Services—primarily from the non-commissioned officer (NCO) and junior officer ranks—USSOCOM will have a smaller force pool to draw its members from. In addition, because the Services will have fewer troops, they might not be as receptive to USSOCOM recruitment efforts in order to keep high-quality NCOs and junior officers in their conventional units. Another implication is that these force reductions might also have an impact on the creation and sustainment of Army and Marine Corps "enabling" units that USSOCOM is seeking to support operations.

Another potential issue involves initiatives to get more "time at home" for SOF troops to help reduce stress on service members and their families. One of the major factors cited by USSOCOM leadership regarding "time away from family" is that SOF does not either have access to or the appropriate types of training facilities near their home stations, thereby necessitating travel away from their bases and families to conduct pre-deployment training. While the creation of additional local SOF training facilities might seem to be an obvious solution to this problem, the availability of land for military use as well as existing environmental regulations could make it difficult for USSOCOM to create new training facilities or modify existing facilities to suit SOF training requirements.

BACKGROUND

Overview

Special Operations Forces (SOF) are elite military units with special training and equipment that can infiltrate into hostile territory through land, sea, or air to conduct a variety of operations, many of them classified. SOF personnel undergo rigorous selection and lengthy specialized training. The U.S. Special Operations Command (USSOCOM) oversees the training, doctrine, and equipping of all U.S. SOF units.

Command Structures and Components

In 1986 Congress, concerned about the status of SOF within overall U.S. defense planning, passed measures (P.L. 99-661) to strengthen special operations' position within the defense community. These actions included the establishment of USSOCOM as a new unified command. USSOCOM is headquartered at MacDill Air Force Base in Tampa, FL. The Commander of USSOCOM is a four-star officer who may be from any military service. The current commander is Navy Admiral Eric T. Olson, who reports directly to the Secretary of Defense, although an Assistant Secretary of Defense for Special Operations and Low Intensity Conflict and Interdependent Capabilities (ASD/SOLIC&IC) provides immediate civilian oversight over many USSOCOM activities.

USSOCOM has about 58,000 active duty, National Guard, and reserve personnel from all four services and Department of Defense (DOD) civilians assigned to its headquarters, its four components, and one sub-unified command.[1] USSOCOM's components are the U.S.

Army Special Operations Command (USASOC); the Naval Special Warfare Command (NAVSPECWARCOM); the Air Force Special Operations Command (AFSOC); and the Marine Corps Special Operations Command (MARSOC). The Joint Special Operations Command (JSOC) is a USSOCOM sub-unified command.

Expanded USSOCOM Responsibilities

In addition to its Title 10 authorities and responsibilities, USSOCOM has been given additional responsibilities. In the 2004 Unified Command Plan, USSOCOM was given the responsibility for synchronizing DOD plans against global terrorist networks and, as directed, conducting global operations against those networks.[2] In this regard, USSOCOM "receives, reviews, coordinates and prioritizes all DOD plans that support the global campaign against terror, and then makes recommendations to the Joint Staff regarding force and resource allocations to meet global requirements."[3] In October 2008, USSOCOM was designated as the DOD proponent for Security Force Assistance (SFA).[4] In this role, USSOCOM will perform a synchronizing function in global training and assistance planning similar to the previously described role of planning against terrorist networks. In addition, USSOCOM is now DOD's lead for countering threat financing, working with the U.S. Treasury and Justice Departments on means to identify and disrupt terrorist financing efforts.

Army Special Operations Forces

U.S. Army SOF (ARSOF) includes approximately 28,500 soldiers from the Active Army, National Guard, and Army Reserve who are organized into Special Forces, Ranger, and special operations aviation units, along with civil affairs units, psychological operations units, and special operations support units. ARSOF Headquarters and other resources, such as the John F. Kennedy Special Warfare Center and School, are located at Fort Bragg, NC. Five active Special Forces (SF) Groups (Airborne),[5] consisting of about 1,400 soldiers each, are stationed at Fort Bragg and at Fort Lewis, WA, Fort Campbell, KY, Fort Carson, CO, and Eglin Air Force Base, FL. Special Forces soldiers—also known as the Green Berets—are trained in various skills, including foreign languages, that allow teams to operate independently throughout the world. In December 2005, the 528th Sustainment Brigade (Special Operations) (Airborne) was activated at Ft. Bragg, NC, to provide combat service support and medical support to Army special operations forces.[6]

In FY2008, the U.S. Army Special Operations Command (USASOC) began to increase the total number of Army Special Forces battalions from 15 to 20, with one battalion being allocated to each active Special Forces Group. In August 2008, the Army stood up the first of these new battalions—the 4th Battalion, 5th Special Forces Groups (Airborne)—at Fort Campbell, KY.[7] The Army expects that the last of these new Special Forces battalions will be operational by FY2013.[8] Two Army National Guard Special Forces groups are headquartered in Utah and Alabama. An elite airborne light infantry unit specializing in direct action operations[9], the 75th Ranger Regiment, is headquartered at Fort Benning, GA, and consists of three battalions. Army special operations aviation units, including the 160th Special Operations Aviation Regiment (Airborne), headquartered at Fort Campbell, KY, feature pilots trained to fly the most sophisticated Army rotary-wing aircraft in the harshest environments, day or night, and in adverse weather.

Some of the most frequently deployed SOF assets are civil affairs (CA) units, which provide experts in every area of civil government to help administer civilian affairs in operational theaters. The 95th Civil Affairs Brigade (Airborne) is the only active CA unit; all other CA units reside in the Reserves and are affiliated with conventional Army units. Military Information Support Operations units disseminate information to large foreign audiences through mass media. The active duty 4th Military Information Support Group (MISO), (Airborne) is stationed at Fort Bragg, and two Army Reserve MISO groups work with conventional Army units.

Air Force Special Operations Forces[10]

The Air Force Special Operations Command (AFSOC) is one of the Air Force's 10 major commands with over 12,000 active duty personnel and over 16,000 personnel when civilians, Guard and Reserve personnel and units are included. While administrative control of AFSOC is overseen by the Chief of Staff of the Air Force (CSAF), operational control is managed by the USSOCOM Commander. AFSOC units operate out of four major continental Unite States (CONUS) locations and two overseas locations. The headquarters for AFSOC, the first Special Operations Wing (1st SOW), and the 720th Special Tactics Group are located at Hurlburt Field, FL. The 27th SOW is at Cannon AFB, NM. The 352nd and 353rd Special Operations Groups provide forward presence in Europe (RAF Mildenhall, England) and in the Pacific (Kadena Air Base, Japan) respectively. The Air National Guard's 193rd SOW at Harrisburg, PA, and the Air Force Reserve Command's 919th SOW at Duke Field, FL, complete AFSOC's major units. A training center, the U.S. Air Force Special Operations School and Training Center (AFSOTC), was recently established and is located at Hurlburt Field. AFSOC conducts the majority of its specialized flight training through an arrangement with Air Education and Training Command (AETC) via the 550th SOW at Kirtland AFB, NM. AFSOC's four active-duty flying units are composed of more than 100 fixed and rotary-wing aircraft.

In March 2009, Headquarters AFSOC declared initial operational capability (IOC)[11] for the CV-22.[12] USSOCOM plans for all 50 CV-22s to be delivered to AFSOC by 2015.[13] Since 2009, AFSOC has completed three overseas deployments, to Central America, Africa, and Iraq, and continues to be engaged currently in overseas contingency operations. Despite critical reviews of the aircraft, AFSOC considers the CV-22 "central to our future."[14] AFSOC operates a diverse fleet of modified aircraft. Of 12 major design series aircrafts, 7 are variants of the C-130, the average age of some of which is over 40 years old and date from the Viet Nam era. Because of the age of the fleet, AFSOC considers recapitalization one of its top priorities.

AFSOC's Special Tactics experts include Combat Controllers, Pararescue Jumpers, Special Operations Weather Teams, and Tactical Air Control Party (TACPs). As a collective group, they are known as Special Tactics and have also been referred to as "Battlefield Airmen." Their basic role is to provide an interface between air and ground forces, and these airmen have very developed skill sets. Usually embedded with Army, Navy, or Marine SOF units, they provide control of air fire support, medical and rescue expertise, or weather support, depending on the mission requirements.

As directed in the 2010 QDR, AFSOC plans to increase aviation advisory manpower and resources resident in the 6th Special Operations Squadron (SOS). The 6th SOS's mission is to assess, train, and advise partner nation aviation units with the intent to raise their capability and capacity to interdict threats to their nation. The 6th SOS provides aviation expertise to U.S. foreign internal defense (FID) missions.

Naval Special Operations Forces[15]

The Naval Special Warfare Command (NSWC) consists of about 8,800 military and civilian personnel and is located in Coronado, CA. NSWC is organized around 10 SEAL Teams, two SEAL Delivery Vehicle (SDV) Teams, and three Special Boat Teams. SEAL Teams consist of six SEAL platoons each, consisting of two officers and 16 enlisted personnel. The major operational components of NSWC include Naval Special Warfare Groups One, Three, and Eleven, stationed in Coronado, CA, and Naval Special Warfare Groups Two and Four and the Naval Special Warfare Development Group in Little Creek, VA. These components deploy SEAL Teams, SEAL Delivery Vehicle Teams, and Special Boat Teams worldwide to meet the training, exercise, contingency and wartime requirements of theater commanders. SEALs are considered the best-trained combat swimmers in the world, and can be deployed covertly from submarines or from sea and land-based aircraft.

Marine Special Operations Command (MARSOC)[16]

On November 1, 2005, DOD announced the creation of the Marine Special Operations Command (MARSOC) as a component of USSOCOM. MARSOC consists of three subordinate units—the Marine Special Operations Regiment, which includes 1st, 2nd, and 3rd Marine Special Operations Battalions; the Marine Special Operations Support Group; the Marine Special Operations Intelligence Battalion; and the Marine Special Operations School. MARSOC Headquarters, the 2nd and 3rd Marine Special Operations Battalions, the Marine Special Operations School, and the Marine Special Operations Support Group and the Marine Special Operations Intelligence Battalion are stationed at Camp Lejeune, NC. The 1st Marine Special Operations Battalion is stationed at Camp Pendleton, CA. MARSOC forces have been deployed worldwide to conduct a full range of special operations activities. By 2014, MARSOC is planned to have about 3,000 marines, sailors, and civilians.

Marine Corps Force Structure Review[17]

In the fall of 2010, the Marines Corps conducted a force structure review that focused on the post Operation Enduring Freedom [Afghanistan] security environment. This review had a number of recommendations for Marine forces, including MARSOC. The review called for strengthening MARSOC by more than 1,000 Marines including a 44% increase in critical combat support and service support Marines. It is currently not known how these proposed increases will translate into additional capabilities and new force structure and how much these proposed additions will cost.

Joint Special Operations Command (JSOC)

According to DOD, the JSOC is "a joint headquarters designed to study special operations requirements and techniques; ensure interoperability and equipment standardization; plan and conduct joint special operations exercises and training; and develop joint special operations tactics."[18] While not officially acknowledged by DOD or USSOCOM, JSOC, which is headquartered at Pope Air Force Base, NC, is widely believed to command and control what are described as the military's special missions units—the Army's Delta Force, the Navy's SEAL Team Six, the 75th Ranger Regiment, the 160th Special Operations Aviation Regiment and the Air Force's 24th Special Tactics Squadron.[19] JSOC's primary mission is believed to be identifying and destroying terrorists and terror cells worldwide.

A recent news release by the U.S. Army Special Operations Command (USASOC) News Service which names Vice Admiral William McRaven as Admiral Olson's successor seemingly adds credibility to press reports about JSOC's alleged counterterrorism mission. The USASOC press release notes: "McRaven, a former commander of SEAL Team 3 and Special Operations Command Europe, is the commander of the Joint Special Operations Command. As such, he has led the command as it "ruthlessly and effectively [took] the fight to America's most dangerous and vicious enemies," Gates said."[20]

NATO Special Operations Headquarters[21]

In May 2010, NATO established the NATO Special Operations Headquarters (NSHQ), which is commanded by U.S. Air Force Lieutenant General Frank Kisner, who had previously commanded U.S. Special Operations Command—Europe (SOCEUR). The NSHQ is envisioned to serve as the core of a combined joint force special operations component command, which would be the proponent for planning, training, doctrine, equipping, and evaluating NATO special operations forces from 22 countries. The NSHQ is located with the Supreme Headquarters Allied Powers Europe (SHAPE) in Mons, Belgium, and will consist of about 150 NATO personnel.

CURRENT ORGANIZATIONAL AND BUDGETARY ISSUES

Pending Change in USSOCOM Leadership[22]

Vice Admiral William McRaven, the current commander of JSOC, has been recommended for nomination to replace Admiral Olson (who is retiring this year) as USSOCOM Commander. From the U.S. Army Special Operations Command News Service:

Defense Secretary Robert M. Gates is recommending that President Barack Obama nominate Vice Adm. William McRaven for a fourth star and to the position of commander, U.S. Special Operations Command. ... Gates made the recommendations during a Pentagon press briefing March 1. If confirmed by the Senate, McRaven would succeed Navy Adm. Eric Olson, who has headed the command since 2008.

2010 Quadrennial Defense Review (QDR) Report SOF-Related Directives[23]

The 2010 QDR contains a number of SOF-related directives pertaining to personnel, organizations, and equipment. These include the following:

- To increase key enabling assets[24] for special operations forces.
- To maintain approximately 660 special operations teams;[25] 3 Ranger battalions; and 165 tilt-rotor/fixed-wing mobility and fire support primary mission aircraft.
- The Army and USSOCOM will add a company of upgraded cargo helicopters (MH-47G) to the Army's 160th Special Operations Aviation Regiment.
- The Navy will dedicate two helicopter squadrons for direct support to naval special warfare units.
- To increase civil affairs capacity organic to USSOCOM.
- Starting in FY2012, purchase light, fixed-wing aircraft to enable the Air Force's 6th Special Operations squadron to engage partner nations for whose air forces such aircraft might be appropriate, as well as acquiring two non-U.S. helicopters to support these efforts.

The significance of these directives are that they serve as definitive goals for USSOCOM growth and systems acquisition as well as directing how the Services will support USSOCOM.

2012 USSOCOM Defense Authorization Request and Posture Hearings[26]

In early March 2011, USSOCOM Commander Admiral Eric T. Olson testified to the Senate and House Armed Service Committees and, in addition to discussing budgetary requirements, also provided an update of the current state of U.S. SOF. Key points emphasized by Admiral Olson included the following:

- USSOCOM totals close to about 60,000 people with about 20,000 of whom are career members of SOF, meaning those who have been selected, trained, and qualified as SOF operators.
- Since September 11, 2001, USSOCOM manpower has nearly doubled, the budget nearly tripled, and overseas deployments have quadrupled. As an example, Admiral Olson noted that as 100,000 US troops came out of Iraq, fewer than 1,000 were from SOF and at the same time there was a requirement to move about 1,500 SOF to Afghanistan. As a result of this high demand for SOF, Admiral Olson stated that

SOF is "fraying around the edges" and "showing signs of wear" but still remains a fundamentally strong and sound force.

- Admiral Olson further noted a slight increase in mid-career special operations troops with 8 to 10 years of service opting to leave the service.
- One of the key actions that USSOCOM is taking is to get SOF more "days at home" and predictability and part of that effort is trying to relieve SOF members of jobs or responsibilities that can be done by other individuals or units.
- One key problem that USOCOM faces that contributes to fewer "days at home" for SOF personnel is the lack of readily available, local ranges so that SOF can conduct pre-deployment training. Such a lack of local ranges means that SOF operators have to "travel to train" which further increases their time away from home.
- USSOCOM is also developing a force generation system that will better interface with the Service's force generation systems which is intended to provide better, more optimized force packages to the Geographic Combatant Commanders.
- Section 1208 authority (Section 1208 of P.L. 108-375, the FY2005 National Defense Authorization Act) provides authority and funds for U.S. SOF to train and equip regular and irregular indigenous forces to conduct counterterrorism operations. Section 1208 is considered a key tool in combating terrorism and is directly responsible for a number of highly successful counter-terror operations.
- Regarding equipment, USSOCOM is fielding the first of 72 planned MH-60M helicopters; is on the path to recapitalize the gunship fleet with AC-130J models; and the MC-130J program is on track to replace aging MC-130Es and MC-130Ps. USSOCOM plans to award a competitive prototype contract later this year for the Combatant Craft-Medium (CCM) to replace the Special Warfare Rigid Hull Inflatable Boat (RHIB) and has also realigned funds from cancelled programs to fund the development of a family of Dry Submersibles that can be launched from surface ships or specialized submarines.

FY2012 USSOCOM Budget Request

USSOCOM's FY2012 Budget Request is $10.5 billion—with $7.2 billion in the baseline budget and $3.3 billion in the Overseas Contingency Operations (OCO) budget.[27] This represents an increase of seven percent over the FY2011 Budget Request of $9.8 billion. USSOCOM has long maintained that it represents about 2% of the Department of Defense budget and provides maximum operational impact for a limited investment. Another one of SOCOM's perceived benefits is that its components take proven, service-common equipment and modify it with SOF funding for special operations-unique capabilities.

POSSIBLE ISSUES FOR CONGRESS

Transition to Iraqi Special Operations Forces[28]

Reports suggest that after years of training by U.S. SOF, Iraqi SOF are now taking the lead in counterterrorism operations in Iraq. The almost 4,100 member Iraqi SOF are now planning and conducting their own missions with U.S. SOF providing some intelligence assistance and post-mission advice. Some maintain that this represents a highly successful effort in building Iraq's indigenous counterterrorism capabilities from the ground up. Congress might examine the lessons learned from training and equipping Iraqi SOF for use in future oversight activities.

Potential Impact of Army and Marine Corps Downsizing[29]

On January 6, 2011, Secretary of Defense Gates and Chairman of the Joint Chiefs of Staff Admiral Mike Mullen announced that starting in FY2015, the Army would decrease its permanently authorized endstrength by 27,000 soldiers and that the Marines would lose anywhere between 15,000 to 20,000 Marines, depending on their force structure review. These downsizings have implications for USSOCOM. The first is that because USSOCOM draws their operators and support troops from the Services (primarily from the non-commissioned officer (NCO) and junior officer ranks) USSOCOM will have a smaller force pool to draw its members from. In addition, because the Service will have fewer troops, they might not be as receptive to USSOCOM recruitment efforts in order to keep high-quality NCOs and junior officers in their current units. Another implication is that these force reductions might also affect the creation and sustainment of Army and Marine Corps "enabling" units that USSOCOM is seeking to support operations. In this particular circumstance, Congress might decide to examine with the Services and USSOCOM how these downsizing efforts might affect the creation of enabling units.

Initiatives to Increase SOF "Days at Home"

Because USSOCOM growth is limited due to the high entrance standards for SOF candidates, while requirements to deploy SOF are likely to continue at the current rate, efforts to increase SOF "days at home" to decrease stress on SOF and their families will probably need to focus on times when SOF units are at their home stations. One of the major factors cited by USSOCOM leadership is that SOF units do not always have access to appropriate training facilities near their home stations, thereby necessitating travel away from their bases to conduct pre-deployment training. Given these circumstances, Congress might act to review USSOCOM proposals to improve the situation, whether by giving SOF priority access to existing training facilities, by modifying existing facilities to accommodate SOF training, or by building new SOF-dedicated training facilities closer to SOF bases. Factors that could limit efforts to improve SOF local training include the availability of land for military use, as

End Notes

[1] Information in this section is from "Fact Book: United States Special Operations Command," USSOCOM Public Affairs, February 2011, p. 7. DOD defines a sub-unified command as a command established by commanders of unified commands, when so authorized through the Chairman of the Joint Chiefs of Staff, to conduct operations on a continuing basis in accordance with the criteria set forth for unified commands. A subordinate unified command may be established on an area or functional basis. Commanders of subordinate unified commands have functions and responsibilities similar to those of the commanders of unified commands and exercise operational control of assigned commands and forces within the assigned joint operations area.

[2] "Fact Book: United States Special Operations Command," USSOCOM Public Affairs, February 2011, p. 4.

[3] Ibid.

[4] Information in this section is from testimony given by Admiral Eric T. Olson, Commander, U.S. SOCOM, to the House Terrorism, Unconventional Threats and Capabilities Subcommittee on the Fiscal Year 2010 National Defense Authorization Budget Request for the U.S. Special Operations Command, June 4, 2009.

[5] Airborne refers to "personnel, troops especially trained to effect, following transport by air, an assault debarkation, either by parachuting or touchdown." Joint Publication 1-02, Department of Defense Dictionary of Military and Associated Terms, 12 April 2001, (As Amended Through 31 July 2010).

[6] "Fact Book: United States Special Operations Command," USSOCOM Public Affairs, February 2011, p. 13.

[7] Sean D. Naylor, "Special Forces Expands," *Army Times,* August 11, 2008.

[8] Association of the United States Army, "U.S. Army Special Operations Forces: Integral to the Army and the Joint Force," *Torchbearer National Security Report,* March 2010, p. 3.

[9] Direct action operations are short-duration strikes and other small-scale offensive actions conducted as a special operation in hostile, denied, or politically sensitive environments, as well as employing specialized military capabilities to seize, destroy, capture, exploit, recover, or damage designated targets. Direct action differs from conventional offensive actions in the level of physical and political risk, operational techniques, and the degree of discriminate and precise use of force to achieve specific objectives.

[10] Information in this section is from Lt Gen Wurster's presentation to the Air Force Association, September 14 2010. http://www.afa.org/events/conference/2010/scripts/Wurster_9-14.pdf and "Fact Book: United States Special Operations Command," USSOCOM Public Affairs, February 2011.

[11] According to DOD IOC is attained when some units and/or organizations in the force structure scheduled to receive a system 1) have received it and 2) have the ability to employ and maintain it.

[12] The CV-22 is the special operations version of the V-22 Osprey tilt-rotor aircraft used by the Marine Corps.

[13] USSOCOM Acquisitions and Logistics office, http://www.socom.mil/soal/Pages/FixedWing.aspx.

[14] For further detailed reporting on the V-22 program, see CRS Report RL31384, *V-22 Osprey Tilt-Rotor Aircraft: Background and Issues for Congress*, by Jeremiah Gertler.

[15] Information in this section is from "Fact Book: United States Special Operations Command," USSOCOM Public Affairs, February 2011, pp. 20-21.

[16] Information in this section is from "Fact Book: United States Special Operations Command," USSOCOM Public Affairs, February 2011, p. 37.

[17] "Reshaping America's Expeditionary Force in Readiness: Report of the 2010 Marine Corps Force Structure Review Group," March 14, 2011.

[18] USSOCOM website http://www.socom.mil/components/components.htm, accessed March 19, 2008.

[19] Jennifer D. Kibbe, "The Rise of the Shadow Warriors," Foreign Affairs, Volume 83, Number 2, March/April 2004 and Sean D. Naylor, "JSOC to Become Three-Star Command," *Army Times*, February 13, 2006.

[20] U.S. Army Special Operations Command News Service, "Gates Nominates McRaven, Thurman for Senior Posts," Release Number: 110303-02, March 3, 2011, http://www.soc.mil/UNS/Releases/2011/March/110303-02.html.

[21] Information in this section is taken from Carlo Mu oz, "SOCEUR Chief Pegged: Air Force Two-Star to Head Up New NATO Special Ops Headquarters," *Inside the Air Force,* May 28, 2010 and NATO Fact Sheet, "NATO Special Operations Headquarters (NSHQ)," accessed from http://www.NATO.int on July 1, 2010.

[22] U.S. Army Special Operations Command News Service, "Gates Nominates McRaven, Thurman for Senior Posts," Release Number: 110303-02, March 3, 2011, http://www.soc.mil/UNS/Releases/2011/March/110303-02.html.

[23] Information in this section is from Department of Defense, Quadrennial Defense Review Report, February 2010.

[24] Enabling assets are a variety of conventional military units that are assigned to support special operations forces.

[25] These teams include Army Special Forces Operational Detachment-Alpha (ODA) teams; Navy Sea, Air, and Land (SEAL) platoons; Marine special operations teams, Air Force special tactics teams; and operational aviation detachments.

[26] CQ Congressional Transcripts, Senate Armed Services Committee Holds Hearings on the Fiscal 2012 Defense Authorization Requests for the U.S. Special Operations Command and the U.S. Central Command, March 1, 2011 and Posture Statement of Admiral Eric T. Olson, USN, Commander, United States Special Operations Command Before the 112th Congress House Armed Services Committee March 3, 2011.

[27] Information in this section is from the United States Special Operations Command FY2012 Budget Estimates, February 2011 and Posture Statement of Admiral Eric T. Olson, USN, Commander, United States Special Operations Command Before the 112th Congress House Armed Services Committee March 3, 2011.

[28] Thomas Erdbrink, "In Iraq, U.S. Special Forces Gearing Up to Leave," *Washington Post,* March 24, 2011.

[29] Unless otherwise noted, information in this section is taken from U.S. Department of Defense News Transcript, "DOD News Briefing with Secretary Gates and Adm. Mike Mullen from the Pentagon" January 6, 2011. http://www.defense.gov/transcripts/transcript.aspx?transcriptid=4747.

In: U.S. Special Operations Forces
Editor: Michael E. Harris and Roger L. Cook

ISBN: 978-1-61470-507-9
© 2011 Nova Science Publishers, Inc.

Chapter 2

USSOCOM FACT BOOK

Special Operations Forces

USSOCOM MISSION

- Provide fully capable Special Operations Forces to defend the United States and its interests.
- Synchronize planning of global operations against terrorist networks.

USSOCOM PRIORITIES

Deter, Disrupt & Defeat Terrorist Threats

- Plan & Conduct Special Operations
- Emphasize Persistent, Culturally Attuned Engagement
- Foster Interagency Cooperation

Develop & Support our People & Families

- Focus on Quality
- Care for our People and Families
- Train & Educate the Joint Warrior/Diplomat

Sustain & Modernize the Force

- Equip the Operator
- Upgrade SOF Mobility
- Obtain Persistent Intelligence, Surveillance & Reconnaissance Systems

SPECIAL OPERATIONS FORCES MEDAL OF HONOR RECIPIENTS

Korea

Army Master Sgt. Ola L. Mize

Vietnam

Army Capt. Humbert Roque Versace
Army Capt. Roger H. C. Donlon
Army 1st Lt. Charles Q. Williams
Air Force Maj. Bernard F. Fisher
Army Capt. Ronald E. Ray
Navy Boatswain's Mate 1st Class James E. Williams
Army 1st Lt. George K. Sisler
Navy Seaman David G. Ouellet
Army Master Sgt. Charles E. Hosking, Jr.
Army Sgt. Gordon D. Yntema
Army Staff Sgt. Drew D. Dix
Army Sgt. 1st Class Eugene Ashley, Jr.
Army Sgt. 1st Class Fred W. Zabitosky
Army Master Sgt. Roy P. Benavidez
Air Force Lt. Col. Joe M. Jackson
Army Specialist 5th Class John J. Kedenburg
Air Force Col. William A. Jones III
Army Staff Sgt. Laszlo Rabel
Air Force Capt. James P. Fleming
Army Specialist 4th Class Robert D. Law
Air Force Airman 1st Class John L. Levitow
Navy Lt. j.g. (SEAL) Joseph R. Kerrey
Army Sgt. 1st Class William M. Bryant
Army Staff Sgt. Robert J. Pruden
Army Staff Sgt. Franklin D. Miller
Army Sgt. Gary B. Beikirch
Army Sgt. 1st Class Gary L. Littrell
Army Sgt. Brian L. Buker
Army Staff Sgt. John R. Cavaiani
Army 1st Lt. Loren D. Hagen
Navy Lt. (SEAL) Thomas R. Norris
Navy Engineman 2nd Class (SEAL) Michael T. Thornton

Somalia

Army Master Sgt. Gary I. Gordon
Army Sgt. 1st Class Randall D. Shughart

Afghanistan

Navy Lt. (Seal) Michael P. Murphy
Army Staff Sgt. Robert Miller

Iraq

Navy Master-at-Arms 2nd Class (SEAL) Michael Monsoor

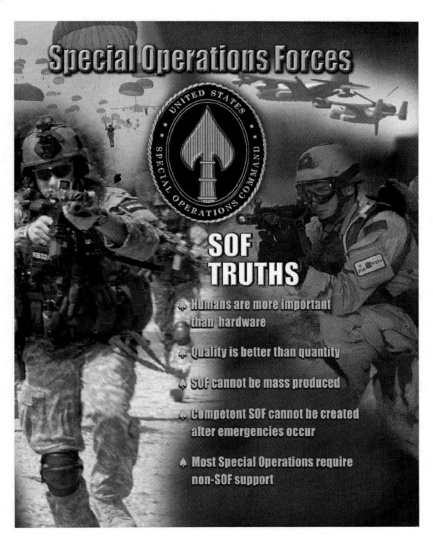

TITLE 10 AUTHORITIES AND RESPONSIBILITIES

- Develop special operations strategy, doctrine and tactics
- Prepare and submit budget proposals for SOF
- Exercise authority, direction and control over special operations expenditures
- Train assigned forces
- Conduct specialized courses of instruction
- Validate requirements
- Establish requirement priorities
- Ensure interoperability of equipment and forces
- Formulate and submit intelligence support requirements
- Monitor Special Operations officers' promotions, assignments, retention, training and professional military education
- Ensure Special Operations Forces' combat readiness
- Monitor Special Operations Forces' preparedness to carry out assigned missions
- Develop and acquire special operations-peculiar equipment, materiel, supplies and services
- Command and control of United States based Special Operations Forces
- Provide Special Operations Forces to the geographic combatant commanders
- Activities specified by the President or SECDEF

SOF CORE ACTIVITIES

Direct Action: Short-duration strikes and other small-scale offensive actions taken to seize, destroy, capture or recover in denied areas.

Special Reconnaissance: Acquiring information concerning the capabilities, intentions and activities of an enemy.

Unconventional Warfare: Operations conducted by, through and with surrogate forces that are organized, trained, equipped, supported and directed by external forces.

Foreign Internal Defense: Providing training and other assistance to foreign governments and their militaries to enable the foreign government to provide for its country's national security.

Civil Affairs Operations: Activities that establish, maintain or influence relations between U.S. forces and foreign civil authorities and civilian populations to facilitate U.S. military operations.

Counterterrorism: Measures taken to prevent, deter and respond to terrorism.

Military Information Support Operations: Operations that provide truthful information to foreign audiences that influence behavior in support of U.S. military operations.

Information Operations: Operations designed to achieve information superiority by adversely affecting enemy information and systems while protecting U.S. information and systems.

Counterproliferation of Weapons of Mass Destruction: Actions taken to locate, seize, destroy or capture, recover and render such weapons safe.

Security Force Assistance: Unified action by joint, interagency, intergovernmental and multinational community to sustain and assist host nation or regional security forces in support of a legitimate authority.

Counterinsurgency Operations: Those military, paramilitary, political, economic, psychological and civic actions taken by a government to defeat insurgency.

Activities Specified by the President or SECDEF

USSOCOM: A BRIEF HISTORY

Two aircraft crashed. Eight servicemembers lost their lives. Fifty-three hostages remained in captivity. Operation Eagle Claw was a heroic effort, but this tragic secret mission in April 1980 showed the need for a joint Special Operations Force, leading to the creation of U.S. Special Operations Command.

The operation occurred at a remote site in Iran known as Desert One, and its purpose was to rescue 53 American hostages held at the U.S. Embassy in Tehran, Iran. Servicemembers from the Army, Navy, Air Force and Marine Corps were involved in the operation, but miscommunication, lack of standardized training among the branches and other external factors caused the mission failure, which showed the need for a unified, multi-service Special Operations command.

Special Operations Forces had declined in the 1970s due to significant SOF funding cuts. Over the next few years following the Desert One disaster, Congress began taking the necessary steps toward building adequate SOF. In 1983, the Senate Armed Services Committee began an in-depth study of the Defense Department, including a careful examination of SOF. When the study was completed two years later, the SASC published a review of its findings entitled, "Defense Organization: The Need for Change." This document, which analyzed past SOF missions and future threats, influenced the creation of the Goldwater-Nichols Act of 1986.

The Goldwater-Nichols Act caused major reorganization throughout the DOD. Shortly after its creation, Congress passed SOF reform bills, calling for a unified combatant command headed by a four-star general for all SOF. The final bill, which amended the Goldwater-

Nichols Act, marked the first time Congress mandated a president create a unified combatant command.

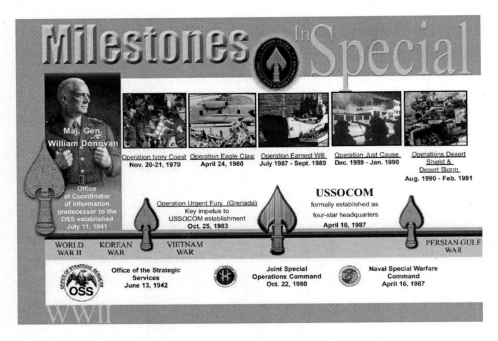

The legislation promised to improve SOF significantly. It fostered joint service cooperation, as a single commander would promote greater interaction among forces within the same command. It also provided SOF with its own resources, allowing the command to modernize forces as needed. Just days after President Ronald Reagan approved the establishment of the new command, the DOD activated USSOCOM April 16, 1987, at MacDill Air Force Base, Fla.

Gen. James A. Lindsay was the first commander of USSOCOM. Since Lindsay, there have been seven other USSOCOM commanders: Generals Carl W. Stiner, Wayne A. Downing, Henry H. Shelton, Peter J. Schoomaker, Charles R. Holland, Bryan D. Brown, and the current commander, Adm. Eric T. Olson, who has held this position since July 2007.

Over the years, USSOCOM's missions and organizational structure have evolved to meet the needs of modern warfare. Originally, the command's mission was "to prepare SOF to carry out missions and, if directed by the President or the Secretary of Defense, to plan and conduct special operations." Commanders refined the mission statement over the years to reflect the need and role of SOF during their periods of time in command. Upon becoming USSOCOM commander, Olson further refined the mission: "Provide fully capable Special Operations Forces to defend the United States and its interests. Plan and synchronize operations against terrorist networks."

SOF deployments have greatly increased since USSOCOM's inception, measured by both personnel deployed and the number of countries visited. Currently, approximately 58,000 servicemembers and civilians work at USSOCOM headquarters or one of its unified commands: U.S. Army Special Operations Command, Naval Special Warfare Command, Air Force Special Operations Command, Marine Corps Forces Special Operations Command, and Joint Special Operations Command, a sub-unified command.

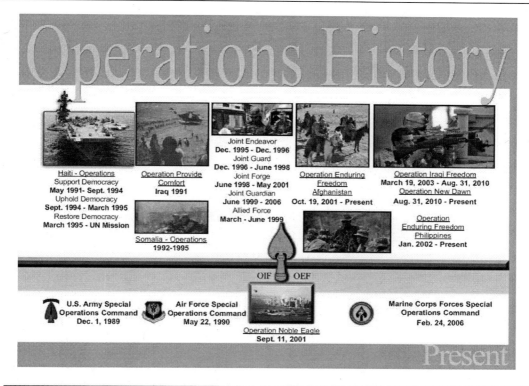

U.S. ARMY SPECIAL OPERATIONS COMMAND

U.S. Army Special Operations Command was established Dec. 1, 1989, by the Department of the Army at Fort Bragg, N.C., as an Army Service Component Command to enhance the readiness of Army Special Operations Forces. USASOC is home to the fighting forces that conduct operations across the full spectrum of warfare, including unconventional warfare, counter-proliferation, direct action, military information support operations, special reconnaissance, civil affairs, foreign internal defense and information operations. USASOC commands and controls two component subordinate commands and five component subordinate units, which in turn train and maintain forces for deployment by USSOCOM to combatant command theaters worldwide.

USASOC's two component subordinate commands are U.S. Army John F. Kennedy Special Warfare Center and School and the U.S. Army Special Forces Command (Airborne) both headquartered at Fort Bragg. The component subordinate units include the 75th Ranger Regiment, headquartered at Fort Benning, Ga.; 160th Special Operations Aviation Regiment (Airborne) at Fort Campbell, Ky.; 4th Military Information Support Group (Airborne), 95th Civil Affairs Brigade (Airborne) and 528th Sustainment Brigade (Special Operations) (Airborne), all at Fort Bragg.

The command also provides oversight of Army National Guard Special Forces' readiness, organization, training and employment in coordination with the National Guard Bureau and state adjutants general.

Known as a world-class Special Operations training center, the **John F. Kennedy Special Warfare Center and School** with more than 600 military and civilian instructors and staff train thousands of agile, adaptive, warrior-focused Soldiers each year. The center and school trains and educates civil affairs, military information support operations and Special Forces Soldiers by providing superior training and education, effective career management and an integrated force-development capability. The center and school leads change based upon today's and ultimately providing an operational force with the most relevant advanced skills necessary to make ARSOF an irreplaceable force.

Spread among seven Special Forces groups, more than 15,000 Soldiers are ever ready, properly trained, oriented and equipped for today's fight. Special Forces warriors are organized, trained and equipped as the right force, fully prepared to support all Geographic Combatant Commanders in a broad spectrum of special operations across the many phases conflict throughout the world.

Rangers are the masters of special light infantry operations. This lethal, agile, and flexible force is capable of executing a wide array of complex joint Special Operations missions across all types of terrain and against our Nation's toughest foes. Their capabilities, responsiveness and reliability define the Ranger Regiment as the versatile and adaptive force of choice for missions of high risk and strategic importance in sensitive or uncertain environments.

Special Operations aviation is a unique unit that organizes, equips, trains, resources and employs Army Special Operations aviation forces worldwide in support of contingency missions and ground force commanders. Known as the Night Stalkers, these Soldiers are recognized for their proficiency in nighttime operations. They are highly trained and ready to accomplish the very toughest missions in all environments, anywhere in the world, day or night, with unparalleled precision.

The mission of **Military Information Support Operations** is to disseminate truthful information to foreign audiences in support of U.S. policy and national objectives. Used during peacetime, contingencies and declared war, these activities are not forms of force, but are force multipliers that use nonviolent means in often violent environments.

In support of Special Operations, **Civil Affairs** units are designed to prevent civilian interference with tactical operations. They provide vital support by working with civil authorities and civilian populations in the area of operations during peace, contingency operations and war. These culturally-oriented, linguistically-capable Soldiers play critical roles in global peace and stabilization and provide support for ongoing missions in various countries.

The **528th Sustainment Brigade** provides logistical, medical and signal services for Army Special Operations Forces worldwide in support of contingency missions. This constantly rotating force ensures Special Operations Forces have what they need to fight and win.

Commander Lt. Gen. John F Mulholland

Senior Enlisted Advisor Command Sgt. Maj. Parry Baer

People

Total Force   Approximately 28,500

Organization

- *U.S. Army John F. Kennedy Special Warfare Center and School – Fort Bragg, N.C.*
  - *1st Special Warfare Training Group (A)*
  - *Special Warfare Medical Group (A)*
- *U.S. Army Special Forces Command (Airborne) – Fort Bragg, N.C.*
  - *1st Special Forces Group (A)*
  - *3rd Special Forces Group (A)*
  - *5th Special Forces Group (A)*
  - *7th Special Forces Group (A)*
  - *10th Special Forces Group (A)*
  - *19th Special Forces Group (A) (Army National Guard)*
  - *20th Special Forces Group (A) (Army National Guard)*
- *75th Ranger Regiment – Fort Benning, Ga.*

- *1st Battalion, 75th Ranger Regiment*
- *2nd Battalion, 75th Ranger Regiment*
- *3rd Battalion, 75th Ranger Regiment*
- *Regimental Special Troops Battalion, 75th Ranger Regiment*
- *160th Special Operations Aviation Regiment (Airborne) – Fort Campbell, KY.*
- *4th Military Information Support Group (Airborne) – Fort Bragg, N.C.*
- *95th Civil Affairs Brigade (Airborne) – Fort Bragg, N.C.*
- *528th Sustainment Brigade (Special Operations) (Airborne) – Fort Bragg, N.C.*

U.S. ARMY JOHN F. KENNEDY SPECIAL WARFARE CENTER AND SCHOOL

The U.S. Army John F. Kennedy Special Warfare Center and School at Fort Bragg, N.C. is one of the Army's premier education institutions, managing and resourcing professional growth for Soldiers in the Army's three distinct Special Operations branches: Special Forces, Civil Affairs and Military Information Support. The Soldiers educated through SWCS programs are using cultural expertise and unconventional techniques to serve their country in and across the globe. More than anything, these Soldiers bring integrity, adaptability and regional expertise to their assignments.

On any given day, approximately 2,200 students are enrolled in SWCS training programs. Courses range from entry-level Special Operations training to advanced warfighter skills for seasoned officers and noncommissioned officers. The 1st Special Warfare Training Group (Airborne) qualifies Soldiers to enter the Special Operations community and teaches them advanced tactical skills as they progress through their careers. The Joint Special Operations Medical Training Center is the central training facility for Department of Defense Special Operations combat medics. Furthermore, SWCS leads efforts to professionalize the Army's entire Special Operations force through the Special Forces Warrant Officer Institute and the David K. Thuma Noncommissioned Officer Academy. While most courses are conducted at Fort Bragg, SWCS enhances its training by maintaining facilities and relationships with outside institutions across the country.

SWCS offers 41 unique courses to give Soldiers the skills they need to survive and succeed on the battlefield.

The Army's Special Operations force is only as good as its education system. Likewise, that education system is only as good as its instructors. By employing the most experienced Soldiers within its units and directorates, SWCS ensures the U.S. Army of tomorrow is equipped with the very best Special Operations force.

SWCS classes and field exercises are led by more than 400 military instructors, each of whom has operated in the same environments or for the same units as their students will. Their real-world experience not only enhances the courses' instruction, but it also fosters camaraderie built on students' and instructors' shared sense of duty and commitment. Annually, one third of the uniformed instructors rotate back to the operational force from which they came in order to maintain operational relevancy in both SWCS and the Army's Special Operations units. Maintaining continuity and providing unique skill-sets are approximately 200 expert civilian instructors and staff members supporting training, doctrine development and publishing initiatives.

Special Operations Soldiers cannot be mass produced and are elite because only the best are selected. As the gateway to the Special Operations community, SWCS selects only the top candidates to even attempt its rigorous training – Soldiers who demonstrate character, commitment, courage and intelligence in their daily lives and professional careers. The Army's Special Operations unit commanders rely on the SWCS directorates to select the strongest candidates and give them the tools to succeed on the battlefield. Using lessons learned from the battlefield, curriculum and doctrine can be amended in a matter of weeks when gaps in training are identified. Together, these directorates oversee administration and policy throughout the community, serving the operational units while allowing them to focus on their missions with full confidence in their Soldiers' preparedness.

Army Special Operations Soldiers have a tremendous impact on today's world, and at each stage in their careers, the U.S. Army John F. Kennedy Special Warfare Center and School is with them to guide and develop their skills.

U.S. Army Special Forces Command [Airborne]

The Army 1st Special Operations Command was redesignated the U.S. Army Special Forces Command (Airborne) Nov. 27, 1990. The mission of USASFC (A) is to organize, equip, train, validate and prepare Special Forces units to deploy and execute operational requirements for the U.S. military's warfighting geographical combatant commanders throughout the world.

Within USASFC (A), there are five active component groups and two U.S. Army National Guard groups. Each group has three line battalions, a group support battalion and a headquarters company. The companies within the line battalions have six Operational Detachment Alphas, or A-teams, assigned to them. The ODA is the heart and soul of SF operations.

Unlike any other divisional-sized unit, USASFC (A) components are not located in one place, but spread out from coast-to-coast and throughout the world.

Each Special Forces Group is regionally oriented to support one of the warfighting geographic combatant commanders. Special Forces Soldiers routinely deploy in support of the GCCs of U.S. European Command, U.S. Pacific Command, U.S. Southern Command, U.S. Central Command and U.S. Africa Command.

Special Forces units perform seven doctrinal missions: unconventional warfare, foreign internal defense, special reconnaissance, direct action, combating terrorism, counter proliferation and information operations. These missions make Special Forces unique in the U.S. military because they are employed throughout the three stages of the operational continuum: peacetime, conflict and war.

Special Forces Command's unconventional warfare capabilities provide a viable military option for a variety of operational taskings that are inappropriate or infeasible for conventional forces, making it the U.S. military's premier unconventional warfare force.

Foreign internal defense operations, SF's main peacetime mission, are designed to help friendly developing nations by working with their military and police forces to improve their technical skills, understanding of human rights issues, and to help with humanitarian and civic action projects.

SF units are often required to perform additional, or collateral, activities outside their primary missions. These collateral activities are coalition warfare/support, combat search and rescue, security assistance, peacekeeping, humanitarian assistance, humanitarian de- mining and counter-drug operations.

On an everyday basis, Soldiers of the U.S. Army Special Forces Command (Airborne) are deployed around the world, living up to their motto – "**De Oppresso Liber**," **To Free the Oppressed**.

75TH RANGER REGIMENT

The 75th Ranger Regiment is a lethal, agile, and versatile Special Operations Force that conducts forcible entry operations and Special Operations raids across the entire spectrum of combat. As the Army's elite Special Operations offensive infantry force, the regiment is capable of planning and executing complex worldwide operations in high- risk, uncertain, and politically sensitive areas. It is constantly transforming to meet future operational requirements without sacrificing mission success.

The regiment's four battalions, geographically dispersed throughout the U.S., can deploy anywhere in the world for no-notice missions. Their capabilities include direct action raids in limited visibility, adverse weather, varied terrain and complex operating environments to capture/kill designated targets and/or seize terrain and strategic installations.

Capable of infiltrating by land, sea or air, the 75th Ranger Regiment is trained on a wide variety of mobility platforms and operates fully integrated with supporting agencies and other Special Operations Forces as required. The unit has an intensive regimental assessment and selection process where only the most exceptional officers, non-commissioned officers, and Soldiers are selected to serve.

From the arduous training to the continuous and demanding worldwide deployments, the Rangers of the 75th Ranger Regiment continue to demonstrate their motto, "Rangers Lead the Way!"

160TH SPECIAL OPERATIONS AVIATION REGIMENT [AIRBORNE]

The 160th Special Operations Aviation Regiment (Airborne), which began as an emergency deployment from Fort Campbell, Ky., in 1980, has evolved into a highly specialized SOF rotary wing aviation capability. The 160th SOAR (A) is USASOC's Special Operations aviation unit specifically manned, equipped and trained to provide precision aviation support to SOF worldwide under any operational and threat environment. To accomplish its mission, the 160th SOAR (A) employs a unique combination of sophisticated, highly modified and combat proven aircraft: MH-60/MH-47/MH-6/AH-6. These aircraft, coupled with the regiment's stringently selected and highly trained aircrews, provide SOF with an ever-expanding array of reliable aviation capabilities. This includes precision rotary wing operations, long-range infiltrations/exfiltration, and performing in adverse weather and all terrain/environmental conditions. The regiment can also conduct long-range precision attack and close-air support for ground SOF and personnel recovery.

4TH MILITARY INFORMATION SUPPORT GROUP [AIRBORNE]

The 4th Military Information Support Group (Airborne), formerly 4th Psychological Operations Group (Airborne), is a vital part of the broad range of U.S. political, military, economic and ideological activities used by the U.S. government to secure national objectives. MISG units develop, produce and disseminate information to foreign audiences in support of U.S. policies and national objectives. Used during peacetime, contingency operations and declared war, these activities are not a form of force, but are force multipliers that use nonviolent means in often violent environments. Persuading rather than compelling physically, the Military Information Support Group rely on logic, fear, desire or other motivational factors to promote specific emotions, attitudes or behaviors. The ultimate objective of U.S. information support operations is to influence target audiences to take actions favorable to the policies of the U.S.

95TH CIVIL AFFAIRS BRIGADE [AIRBORNE]

Civil Affairs Soldiers enable military commanders and U.S. ambassadors to build and maximize relationships with various stakeholders in a local area to meet the objectives of the U.S. government. Civil Affairs teams work with U.S. Department of State country teams, government and non-governmental organizations at all levels and with local populations in peaceful, contingency and hostile environments.

Civil Affairs units may rapidly deploy to remote areas as well as to larger population centers in countries around the world. They help host nations assess the needs of an area, bring together local and non-local resources to ensure long-term stability, and ultimately degrade and defeat violent extremist organizations and their ideologies. They may be involved in disaster prevention, management and recovery, and with human and civil infrastructure assistance programs.

Civil Affairs Soldiers are Soldiers first, but are adept at working in foreign environments and conversing in one of approximately 20 foreign languages with local stakeholders. They may work for months or years in remote areas of a host nation. Their low profile and command structure allow them to solidify key relationships and processes to address root causes of instability that adversely affect the strategic interests of the United States.

58TH SUSTAINMENT BRIGADE [SPECIAL OPERATIONS] [AIRBORNE]

Formerly the Sustainment Brigade (Special Operations) (Airborne), the 528th Sustainment Brigade (Special Operations) (Airborne) assumed the lineage of the 528th Support Battalion. As part of the overall Army Special Operations Forces logistics transformation, the 528th Sustainment Brigade (Special Operations) (Airborne) sets the operational level logistics conditions to enable ARSOF operations worldwide using three Support Operations Teams, two Special Operations Resuscitation Teams, and five Liaison Elements that on order deploy to provide logistical command and control capability. The 528th Sustainment Brigade (Special Operations) (Airborne) plans, coordinates and provides operational and tactical communications for Army Special Operations Task Force commanders with the 112th Special Operations Signal Battalion (Airborne). During the past few years, the brigade has transformed from a unit that does not typically deploy to one constantly rotating into the field to make sure Special Operations Forces have what they need to accomplish mission objectives.

NAVAL SPECIAL WARFARE COMMAND

Naval Special Warfare Command is the maritime component of U.S. Special Operations Command. Established at Naval Amphibious Base, Coronado, Calif., in April 1987, NAVSPECWARCOM's mission is to organize, train, man, equip, educate, sustain, maintain combat readiness and deploy Naval Special Warfare Forces to accomplish Special Operations missions worldwide. NSW Forces operate independently or in conjunction with other SOF, allied units and coalition forces.

A tactical force with strategic impact, NSW mission areas include special reconnaissance, direct action, unconventional warfare, combating terrorism, foreign internal defense, information warfare, security assistance, counterdrug operations, personnel recovery and hydrographic reconnaissance. NSW core training is focused on strategic reconnaissance and direct action — critical skills needed to combat current and future terrorists threats.

Naval Special Warfare Groups are major commands that train, equip and deploy components of NSW squadrons to meet the exercise, contingency and wartime requirements of geographic combatant commanders, Theater Special Operations Commands and numbered fleets located around the world. Two logistical support units are responsible for equipping the teams, and two detachments assume responsibility for individual, unit and squadron-level training. This allows NSW Operators to maintain a strong operational focus.

Naval Special Warfare Combat Service Support Teams provide full-spectrum logistics support to SEAL (sea, air, land) Teams, Special Boat Teams, NSW Task Groups/Task Units. Tasking for each CSST includes crisis-action and logistics planning and coordination, in-theater contracting, small purchase and leasing actions, and comprehensive forward operating base support.

Naval Special Warfare Center provides basic and advanced instruction and training in maritime Special Operations to U.S. military and government personnel and members of select foreign armed forces. NSWC is responsible for the oversight of all courses that lead to individual SEAL and Special Warfare Combatant-craft Crewmen qualifications or certifications.

Naval Special Warfare Development Group, located in Little Creek, Va., manages the test, evaluation and development of technology applicable to Naval Special Warfare forces. The command also develops maritime ground and airborne tactics for Naval Special Warfare and Defense Department-wide application.

Commander *Rear Admiral Edward G. Winters, III*

Senior Enlisted Advisor *Force Master Chief Petty Officer (SEAL) Steven D. Studdard*

People

Total Force   *Approximately 8,800*

Organization

- *Naval Special Warfare Command (NAVSPECWARCOM) — Coronado, Calif.*
- *Naval Special Warfare Group 1 — Coronado, Calif.*
  - *LOGSUPPU 1 — Coronado, Calif.*
  - *SEAL Teams 1/3/5/7 — Coronado, Calif.*
  - *NSWU 1 — Guam*
  - *NSWU 3 — ASU Bahrain*

- *Naval Special Warfare Group 2 – Little Creek, Va.*
  - *LOGSUPPU2 — Little Creek, Va.*
  - *SEAL Teams 2/4/8/10 — Little Creek Va.*
  - *NSWU 2 — Stuttgart, Germany*
  - *NSWU-2 Det. South — Little Creek, Va.*
- *Naval Special Warfare Group 3 – Coronado, Calif.*
  - *SEAL Delivery Vehicle Team 1 — Pearl City, Hawaii*

  - *SEAL Delivery Vehicle Det. 2 Little Creek, Va.*
- *Naval Special Warfare Group 4*
  - *Special Boat Team 20 — Little Creek, Va.*
  - *Special Boat Team 12 — Coronado, Calif.*
  - *Special Boat Team 22 – Stennis, Miss.*
  - *NAVSCIATTS — Stennis, Miss.*
- *Naval Special Warfare Group 11*
  - *SEAL Team 17 — Coronado, Calif.*
  - *SEAL Team 17 — Little Creek, Va.*
- *Naval Special Warfare Center – Coronado, Calif.*
  - *Advanced Training Command — Imperial Beach, Calif.*
  - *Basic Training Command — Coronado, Calif.*
- *Naval Special Warfare Development Group — Dam Neck, Va.*

SEALS [Sea, Air, Land]

The SEAL Team is the heart of the NSW force; a multipurpose combat force organized and trained to conduct a variety of Special Operations missions in all environments. SEALs conduct clandestine missions infiltrating their objective areas by fixed- and rotary-wing aircraft, Navy surface ships, combatant craft, submarines and ground mobility vehicles.

Special Boat Teams

Special Boat Teams are manned by Special Warfare Combatant-craft Crewmen who operate and maintain state-of-the-art surface craft to conduct coastal patrol and interdiction and support special operations missions. Focusing on infiltration and exfiltration of SEALs and other SOF, SWCCs provide dedicated rapid mobility in shallow water areas where larger ships cannot operate. They also bring to the table a unique SOF capability: Maritime Combatant Craft Aerial Delivery System — the ability to deliver combat craft via parachute drop.

SEAL Delivery Vehicle Teams

SEAL Delivery Vehicle Teams are specially trained SEALs and support personnel who conduct undersea operations from SDVs and Dry Deck Shelters. DDSs deliver SDVs and specially trained forces from modified submarines. When teamed with their host submarines, SDV platforms provide the most clandestine maritime delivery capability in the world.

Maritime Surface Platforms

Rigid-hull Inflatable Boat

The Rigid-hull Inflatable Boat performs short-range insertion and extraction of SOF, limited coastal patrol, and interdiction and reconnaissance. The RHIB is a high performance combatant craft that is air transportable by C-5 Galaxy, C-17 Globemaster and C-130 Hercules aircraft, and it can be air dropped from C-130 or larger military aircraft. Each craft is manned by a crew of three Special Warfare Combatant-craft Crewmen and can carry eight SOF personnel.

Special Operations Craft-Riverine

The Special Operations Craft-Riverine performs short-range insertion and extraction of SOF in riverine and littoral environments. The SOC-R is a high-performance craft sized to permit air transport aboard C-130 or larger military aircraft. Each craft is manned by a crew of four Special Warfare Combatant-craft Crewmen and can carry eight SOF personnel.

MK V Special Operations Craft

The MK V Special Operations Craft performs medium-range infiltration and extraction of SOF, limited coastal patrol and interdiction in low to medium threat environments. The MK V SOC is a high-performance combatant craft sized to permit air deployment aboard C-5 aircraft. Each craft is manned by a crew of five Special Warfare Combatant-craft Crewmen and can carry 16 SOF personnel.

GROUND MOBILITY PLATFORMS

Mine Resistant/Ambush Protected Vehicle

The SOCOM employed MRAP is a vehicle with similar handling capabilities as the GMV-N but has been specifically developed to protect the crew from explosive events. The v-hull is designed to survive direct blasts and prevent the crew inside from suffering severe injuries. The weapons system in the turret is remote-operated from inside the cabin, eliminating the exposed gunner position. The MRAP can carry up to eight combat-ready Operators.

Ground Mobility Vehicle – Navy

The GMV-N is a SEAL-specific humvee that employs a multitude of weapons and is fitted with a modular armor kit. Depending on the mission, armor can be added or removed to either increase speed and maneuverability or increase protection. The GMV-N can carry up to five Operators into some of the harshest terrain in the world. Every member of a SEAL team completes an intensive, four-week tactical ground mobility training course where they learn the limitations of the vehicle, basic maintenance and tactical driving skill sets.

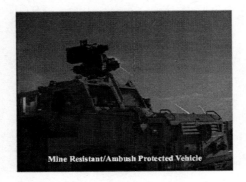
Mine Resistant/Ambush Protected Vehicle

Ground Mobility Vehicle - Navy

UNDERSEA PLATFORMS

SEAL Delivery Vehicle

The MK VIII MOD 1 SEAL Delivery Vehicle is a free-flooding wet submersible designed for undersea special operations including direct action, hydrographic reconnaissance and insertion/extraction of SEALs. It uses a Doppler Navigation Sonar and forward-looking obstacle avoidance sonar to navigate through the water and an underwater telephone with secure, unsecure and data modes to communicate. SDVs can be inserted into the water via a DDS-equipped submarine, MK V SOC or surface ships.

SEAL Delivery Vehicle

MK VIII MOD SEAL Delivery Vehicle and Dry Deck Shelter

The Dry Deck Shelter is a floodable pressure vessel carried by a host submarine for undersea operations. A minimum crew of six Navy divers operates the controls for flooding, draining and pressurizing the DDS. The host submarine provides the DDS with electrical power and high-pressure air. The DDS can be used to launch and recover a SEAL Delivery Vehicle or to conduct mass swimmer lock-out/lock-in operations utilizing SEALs and Combat Rubber Raiding Craft. The divers who operate the DDS control assist in all launch and recovery operations.

AIR FORCE SPECIAL OPERATIONS COMMAND

Air Force Special Operations Command, located at Hurlburt Field, Fla., was established May 22, 1990. AFSOC, the air component to USSOCOM, presents combat-ready Air Force Special Operations Forces to conduct and support global special operations missions. AFSOF is comprised of uniquely trained active duty, Air Force Reserve and Air National Guard personnel. The total force is rapidly deployable and equipped with highly specialized and modified aircraft. AFSOC Air Commandos deliver the Nation's specialized airpower to provide SOF mobility, intelligence support, forward presence and engagement with coalition partners.

AFSOC missions include close-air support/precision firepower, infiltration, exfiltration, resupply, aerial refueling, air/ground interface (Battlefield Airmen), aviation foreign internal defense, intelligence support to special operations (including unmanned aerial surveillance), information operations and airborne radio and television broadcast for military information support operations.

Commander *Lt. Gen. Donald C. Wurster*

Senior Enlisted Advisor *Command Chief Master Sergeant Michael P. Gilbert*

People

Total Force   Approximately 16,000

Organization

- *23rd Air Force – Hurlburt Field, Fla.*

- *1st Special Operations Wing – Hurlburt Field, Fla.*
  - *AC-130U*
  - *CV-22*
  - *MC-130H/P*
- *27th Special Operations Wing – Cannon Air Force Base, N.M.*
  - *MC-130W*
  - *MQ-1*
  - *AC-130H*
- *352nd Special Operations Group — RAF Mildenhall, England*
  - *MC-130H*
  - *MC-130P*
- *353rd Special Operations Group — Kadena Air Base, Japan*
  - *MC-130H*
  - *MC-130P*
- *720th Special Tactics Group — Hurlburt Field, Fla,*
- *Air Force Special Operations Training Center — Hurlburt Field, Fla.*

AFSOC SPECIAL TACTICS

Special Tactics, AFSOC's Battlefield Airmen, is composed of combat control, pararescue, special operations weather and Tactical Air Control Party personnel capable of providing terminal guidance for weapons, control of assault zone aircraft, fire support, mission planning, medical and weather support. Special Tactics Teams frequently operate with Navy SEALs, Army Rangers and Special Forces in direct action, airfield seizure and personnel recovery missions in hostile territory.

THE AIR FORCE SPECIAL OPERATIONS TRAINING CENTER

The Air Force Special Operations Training Center is a primary support unit of AFSOC. Its mission is to recruit, assess, select, indoctrinate, train and educate Air Commandos, other Special Operations Forces and SOF enablers. These missions include aircrew qualification, special tactics, Combat Aviation Advisor and courses conducted at the Air Force Special Operations School.

The Air Force Special Operations School offers focused education in irregular warfare, regional studies and cultural awareness, Special Operations Forces professional development to educate Air Commandos, the special operations community, services and other U.S. government agencies.

The Special Tactics Training Squadron conducts advanced skills training for Combat Controllers, Pararescuemen and Special Tactics officers before they depart for operational special tactics squadrons. The STTS mission will expand to train Special Operations Weathermen, medical field skills, advanced skills for Special Operations Security Forces, integrated combat skills for Combat Aviation Advisors, and Tactical Air Control Party Airmen.

In July 2009, STTS established STTS Det 1 in Yuma, Ariz., to execute the Special Operations Tactical Air Control Course, recently transferred from U.S. Army Special Operations Command to AFSOC to conduct Joint training for SOCOM's Terminal Attack Controllers.

The 19th Special Operations Squadron is an advanced weapons instruction and mission rehearsal unit and is AFSOC's formal school for AC-130U, PC-12, U-28, MC-130E and Combat Aviation Advisors for UH-1, MI-17, and C-130E. The squadron teaches more than 1,100 classes in 70 distinct syllabi of instruction for initial mission qualification, instructor upgrade and continuation refresher training. As a Total Force Initiative, the 5th Special Operations Squadron (Air Force Reserve) has an associate relationship with the 19th SOS with the mission of providing basic aircrew training for U-28 and Combat Aviation Advisor aircrews.

A total force integration effort, the AFSOTC brings together the strengths of active duty, Reserve, Air National Guard, Department of Defense civilians and contract personnel to form an integrated education team dedicated to training new Air Commandos and building warrior ethos to navigate uncertain times ahead.

AFSOTC's newest squadron, the 371st Special Operations Combat Training Squadron, was activated August 13, 2010.

The 371st SOCTS is the AFSOC formal school for Small Unmanned Aerial Systems and Irregular Warfare integrated skills training. The squadron is responsible for specialized training of combat-ready, joint Special Operations Forces and is AFSOC's designated agent for all recruiting, assessment, and selection of Battlefield Airmen and designated SOF aircrew members. The 371st SOCTS also conducts distributed mission operations and mission rehearsal in support of joint and multinational users and provides training support to all AFSOTC-gained units.

The unit's main base is Hurlburt Field, Fla., with the SUAS Joint Flight Training Unit located at Navy Outlying Landing Field Choctaw, Fla.

The 551st Special Operations Squadron is AFSOC's Formal Training Unit at Cannon Air Force Base, N.M. The unit provides aircrew training at AFSOC's newest base to include AC-130H, M-28, Q-200, Dornier 328, MC-130W and MQ-1/9 Remotely Piloted Aircraft.

The 745th Special Operations Squadron is a joint force provider for Air Force Special Operations Command and U.S. Special Operations Command. This flying training unit provides initial and mission qualification training for Air National Guard, U.S. Air Force, and U.S. Navy aircrew in the RC-26 aircraft. The 745th SOS organizes, trains and equips personnel for global deployments providing regional commanders with a highly capable Search and Rescue platform and immediate short-range airlift.

AIR FORCE SPECIAL OPERATIONS SPECIALTIES

Combot Aciation Advisors

Combat Aviation Advisors of the 6th Special Operations Squadron help U.S. global partners to wield airpower. These Air Commandos are culturally savvy, linguistically trained and politically astute Airmen, hand selected for their skill, maturity and professionalism to advise foreign forces in rotary and fixed-wing combat aviation, maintenance, base support, security and tactics. They execute the aviation foreign internal defense mission and train foreign units in specialized and unconventional tactics. The 6th SOS is the only combat aviation advisory unit in DoD. Every day, the 6th SOS has Air Commandos deployed to any given theater of the globe and maintains instructor qualifications on numerous foreign-made aircraft.

Combat Controllers

Combat Controllers are Special Operators and certified air traffic controllers who are an integral part of the Air Force Battlefield Airmen team. Their motto, "First There," indicates the CCT commitment to be the first deployed into restricted environments by air, land or sea to establish assault zones. The assault zone is a drop zone for parachute operations, a landing zone for fixed-wing or helicopter operations, or an extraction zone for low altitude resupply. They set up navigational aid equipment anywhere in the world to guide aircraft for landing on austere runways without the benefit of a tower or large communications system. CCT also control air attacks from all military services aircraft. In addition, CCT provide vital command and control, intelligence gathering, surveying capabilities, limited weather observations and are qualified in demolition to clear hazards and obstructions from runways and landing zones.

Pararescuemen

Pararescuemen, commonly known as PJs, are the only Defense Department specialty specifically trained and equipped to conduct conventional and unconventional recovery operations. A PJ's primary function is as a personnel recovery specialist with emergency trauma medical capabilities in humanitarian and combat environments. They deploy in any available manner, from any available platform, to include air-land-sea tactics, into restricted environments to contact, authenticate, extract, treat, stabilize and evacuate injured personnel, while acting in an enemy-evading, recovery role. PJs participate in combat search and rescue, peacetime search and rescue, protection of the president of the United States, and conduct other operations at the commander's direction. Their motto, "That Others May Live," reaffirms the Pararescueman's commitment to saving lives and self- sacrifice.

Special Operations Weathermen

Special Operations Weathermen are Air Force weather technicians with unique training to operate in hostile or denied territory. They gather, assess, and interpret weather and environmental intelligence from forward deployed locations, working with Special Operations Forces. They collect weather, river, snow, ocean, and terrain intelligence, assist mission planning, generate accurate mission-tailored target and route forecasts in support of global special operations and train joint force members and coalition partners to take and communicate limited weather observations. Additionally, Special Operations Weathermen conduct special reconnaissance, collect upper air data, organize, establish and maintain weather data reporting networks, determine host nation meteorological capabilities and train foreign national forces. Every Special Operations Forces mission is planned using the intelligence and coordination of Special Operations Weathermen.

AIR FORCE SPECIAL OPERATIONS AIRCRAFT

AC-130H/U

Primary function: Close-air support, air interdiction and force protection. **Speed:** 300 mph. **Dimensions:** Wingspan 132 ft. 7 in.; length 97 ft. 9 in.; height 38 ft. 6 in. **Range:** 1,496 mph; unlimited with air refueling. **Armament:** AC-130H, 20 mm Vulcan cannons, 40 mm Bofors cannon and 105 mm Howitzer. AC-130U, 30 mm Bushmaster cannon replacing 25 mm Gatling gun, 40 mm Bofors cannon and 105 mm cannon. **Crew:** AC-130H, 14, and AC-130U, 13.

CV-22A Osprey

Primary function: Special Operations Forces longrange infiltration, exfiltration and re-supply. **Speed:** 277 mph (cruising speed). **Dimensions:** Wingspan 84 ft. 7 in.; length 57 ft. 4 in; height 22 ft. 1 in.; rotary diameter, 38 ft. **Range:** 2,100 miles with internalauxiliary fuel tanks and no refueling. Crew: Four.

EC-130J Commando Solo

Primary function: Psychological and information operations. **Dimensions:** Wingspan 132 ft. 6 in.; length 97 ft.; height 38 ft. 8 in. **Speed:** 335 mph. **Range:** 2,300 miles unrefueled. **Crew:** Ten.

MC-130E/H Combat Talon

Primary function: Infiltration, exfiltration and resupply of special operations forces. **Speed:** 300 mph. **Dimensions:** Wingspan 132 ft. 7 in.; length MC-130E 100 ft. 10 in.; MC-130H 99 ft. 9 in.; height 38 ft. 6 in. **Range:** 2,700 miles unrefueled. **Crew:** MC-130E, nine; MC-130H, seven.

MC-130P Combat Shadow

Primary function: Air refueling special operations forces helicopters. **Speed:** 289 mph. **Dimensions:** Wingspan 132 ft. 7 in.; length 98 ft. 9 in.; height 38 ft. 6 in. **Range:** 4,000 miles unrefueled. **Crew:** Eight

MC-130W Combat Spear

Primary function: Infiltration, exfiltration and resupply of Special Operations Forces; in-flight refueling of special operations vertical lift aircraft. **Speed:** 300 mph. **Dimensions:**

Wingspan 132 ft. 7 in.; length 98 ft. 9 in.; height 38 ft. 6 in. **Range:** 1,208 miles unrefueled. **Crew:** Seven.

U-28A

Primary function: Provide suppport to Special Operations Forces. **Speed:** 359 mph. **Dimensions:** Wingspan 57 ft. 11 in.; length 46 ft. 8 in.; height 14 ft. 4 in. **Range:** 350, 1,700 miles 350ER 2,700 miles. **Crew:** Two.

AFSOC Unmanned Aircraft Systems

Battlefield Air Targeting Micro Air Vehicle (BATMAV)

Primary function: Provides day/night reconnaissance and surveillance with low altitude operation. **Speed:** 20-40 mph. **Dimensions:** Wingspan 28.5 inches; length 10 inches. Operating altitude: 150 to 500 feet.

MQ-1 Predator

Primary function: Armed reconnaissance, airborne surveillance and target acquisition. **Speed:** Up to 135 mph. **Dimensions:** Wingspan 48 ft. 7 in.; length 27 ft.; height 6 ft. 9 in. **Range:** 454 miles. **Armament:** AGM-114 Hellfire missiles.

MQ-9 Reaper

Primary function: Unmanned hunter/killer weapon system. **Speed:** 230 mph. **Dimensions:** Wingspan 66 ft.; length 36 ft.; height 12.5 ft. **Range:** 3,682 miles. **Armament:** AGM-114 Hellfire missiles; GBU-12, GBU-38 JDAM. **Crew:** Pilot and sensor operator on the ground.

MARINE CORPOS FORCES SPECIAL OPERATIONS COMMAND

Headquartered at Camp Lejeune, N.C., the U.S. Marine Corps Forces, Special Operations Command is the Marine Corps component of U.S. Special Operations Command. MARSOC trains, organizes, equips, and, when directed by the Commander USSOCOM, deploys task organized, scalable and responsive Marine Corps Special Operations Forces worldwide in support of combatant commanders and other agencies. MARSOC teams consistently create strategic impacts because its Marines are armed with regionally focused language skills, cultural understanding, and state-of- the-art equipment.

In October 2005, the Secretary of Defense directed the Marine Corps to form a service component of USSOCOM and begin providing forces to the commander of USSOCOM. Formally established Feb. 24, 2006, MARSOC's initial manpower authorization is approximately 2,600 Marines, Sailors and civilian employees.

MARSOC includes three subordinate commands: the Marine Special Operations Regiment, Marine Special Operations Support Group, and the Marine Special Operations School.

MARSOC performs the following missions:

- Direct Action
- Special Reconnaissance
- Security Force Assistance
- Counterinsurgency
- Foreign Internal Defense
- Counterterrorism
- Information Operations
- Civil Affairs
- Military Support Operations
- Counter Proliferation Operations

Commander Maj. Gen. Paul E. Lefebvre

Senior Enlisted Advisor Sergeant Major Richard W. Ashton

People

Total Force   Approximately 2,600

Organization

- The Marine Special Operations Regiment — Camp Lejeune, N.C.
  - 1st Marine Special Operations Battalion — Camp Pendleton, CA
  - 2nd Marine Special Operations Battalion — Camp Lejeune, N.C.
  - 3rd Marine Special Operations Battalion — Camp Lejeune, N.C.
- Marine Special Operations Support Group — Camp Lejeune, N. C.
- Marine Special Operations Intelligence Battalion — Camp Lejeune, N. C.
- Marine Special Operations School — Camp Lejuene, N. C.

MARSOC Personnel

MARSOC is responsible for finding the appropriate personnel for service in three groups: Critical Skills Operators, Direct Combat Support and Combat Service Support.

Critical Skills Operator

Critical Skills Operators are the front line Marines and Sailors who are complex problem solvers able to operate across the full spectrum of Special Operations in small teams under ambiguous, sometimes austere, environments while maintaining a high level of mental flexibility and physical endurance. CSOs exemplify the Marine Corps' concepts of Distributed Operations and the Strategic Corporal.

Direct Combat Support

Direct Combat Support are those Marines who have specialized training in areas including electronic intelligence, communications, logistics, combat skills, fire support, and explosive ordnance disposal. These Marines deploy alongside Marine Special Operations Teams and DCS personnel must meet the same screening requirements as Critical Skill Operators.

Combat Service Support

Combat Service Support personnel are the active- duty and Reserve Marines who fill Combat Service Support billets within MARSOC. These billets range from administrative support to motor transport maintenance.

MARSOC Command and Control

The wide range of missions assigned to Marine Special Operations Forces requires a high level of flexibility and the ability to operate within various command structures. MARSOF can work unilaterally under the Marine Special Operations Regiment, as part of a Joint Special Operations Task Force, as a Special Operations Task Force or as part of a Marine Corps component of a Joint Task Force.

MARSOC Units

Marine Special Operations Regiment

The Marine Special Operations Regiment is located at Camp Lejeune, N.C., and consists of a Headquarters Company and three Marine Special Operations Battalions. The MSOR, which is led by a Marine Corps colonel, provides tailored military combat-skills training and advisor support for identified foreign forces in order to enhance their tactical capabilities and to prepare the environment as directed by USSOCOM as well as the capability to form the nucleus of a Joint Special Operations Task Force. Marines and Sailors of the MSOR train, advise and assist friendly host nation forces - including naval and maritime military and paramilitary forces - to enable them to support their government's internal security and stability, to counter subversion and to reduce the risk of violence from internal and external threats. MSOR deployments are coordinated by MARSOC, through USSOCOM, in accordance with engagement priorities for overseas contingency operations.

Marine Special Operations Battalion

There are three Marine Special Operations Battalions within the MSOR: 1st MSOB located at Camp Pendleton, Calif., and 2d and 3d MSOBs located at Camp Lejeune, N.C. Each MSOB is commanded by a Marine Corps lieutenant colonel and organized, trained and equipped to deploy for worldwide missions as directed by MARSOC. MSOBs are comprised of Marine Special Operations Companies and task- organized with personnel uniquely skilled in special equipment support, intelligence and fire support.

Marine Special Operations Company

Each Marine Special Operations Company is commanded by a Marine Corps Major and is capable of deploying task-organized expeditionary Special Operations Forces to conduct special reconnaissance and direct action missions in support of the geographic combatant commanders. When deployed, each MSOC is augmented with a direct intelligence and enabler capability. The enabling capabilities include a vast array of support ranging from explosive ordnance disposal to military dog handlers.

Marine Special Operations Team

Each Marine Special Operations Team is comprised of 14 Marines and is the backbone of MARSOF. An MSOT can conduct operations in remote areas and austere environments for extended periods with minimal external direction and support. The teams help develop, organize, equip, train, and advise or direct indigenous forces. MSOTs conduct Foreign Internal Defense and other SOF disciplines tasked to MARSOC. Each team has a robust language capability and direct intelligence links to the MSOC as well as access to the company's enabling assets.

Marine Special Operations Support Group

The Marine Special Operations Support Group is lead by a Marine Corps Colonel and is tasked to train, equip, structure, and provide specially qualified Marine forces, including operational logistics, intelligence, Military Working Dogs, Firepower Control Teams and communications support in order to sustain worldwide special operations missions.

Marine Special Operations Intelligence Battalion

On Jan. 1, 2010, MARSOC established Marine Special Operations Intelligence Battalion. The newly created battalion was formed to train, sustain, maintain combat readiness and provide task-organized intelligence support at all operational levels in order to support MARSOF.

Marine Special Operations School

The Marine Special Operations School screens, assesses, selects, and trains Marines and Sailors for special operations assignments in MARSOC; provides both initial and advanced individual special operations training; plans and executes the component exercise program; and serves as MARSOC's training and education proponent in support of MARSOC requirements. MSOS is headed by a Marine Corps colonel.

MSOS is tasked to:

- Conduct a formal Assessment and Selection program
- Conduct an entry-level special operations training course to train NCOs and company grade officers for special operations assignments within MARSOC
- Conduct MARSOC's component exercise program
- Conduct special operations advanced and specialty courses
- Develop MARSOF standards, doctrine and Tactics, Techniques and Procedures
- Serve as MARSOC's proponent for weapons and optics requirements
- Serve as the training and education link between MARSOC, USMC and SOCOM component SOF schools to support MARSOC requirements
- Conduct Advanced Linguist Courses
- Conduct Advanced Skill Courses

USSOCOM SUBORDINATES SPECIAL OPERATIONS COMMANDS

Established in 1980, the **Joint Special Operations Command** is a sub-unified command of USSOCOM. JSOC provides a joint headquarters to study Special Operations requirements, ensures interoperability and equipment standardization, develops joint Special Operations plans and tactics, and conducts joint Special Operations exercises and training.

The Joint Special Operations University resides at MacDill Air Force Base, Fla. JSOU's mission is to educate Special Operations Forces executive, senior and intermediate leaders and selected other national and international security decision-makers, both military and civilian, through teaching, research and outreach in the science and art of Joint Special Operations.

As a Joint Subordinate Command within USSOCOM, the **Joint Military Information Support Command** serves as a key contributor in the Department of Defense's ongoing efforts to erode adversary power, will and influence. JMISC is responsible to plan, coordinate, integrate, and when directed, execute trans-regional influence over relevant populations in support of Combatant Commands, the Secretary of Defense and select government agencies to achieve operational, strategic and national goals and objectives. The senior-level military and DOD civilians who compose the organization include: military information support operations specialists, strategic and regional intelligence analysts, behavioral scientists, cultural advisors, media experts and multi-media product developers. The JMISC provides the DOD with a dynamic, responsive and sophisticated influence capability that plans, coordinates and manages the execution of trans-regional information programs in support of the DOD and regional security objectives.

Theater Special Operations Commands

Joint Forces Command and each geographic combatant command have a Special Operations component commander just like it has a ground, air and naval component commander. The commander of the Theater Special Operations Command is responsible for commanding all SOF in the theater to which the TSOC is assigned. The TSOC is a sub-unified command of the geographic combatant command and the source of expertise in all areas of Special Operations. The TSOC provides the geographic combatant commanders with a separate element to plan and control joint SOF in their theaters.

SOCCENT

Special Operations Command Central, headquartered at MacDill Air Force Base, is a subordinate unified command of U.S. Central Command. It is responsible for planning Special Operations throughout the USCENTCOM area of responsibility, planning and conducting peacetime joint/combined Special Operations training exercises and orchestrating command and control of peacetime and wartime Special Operations as directed. SOCCENT exercises operational control of assigned and attached SOF that deploy for the execution of training and for operational missions in the USCENTCOM AOR as directed by the USCENTCOM commander. When directed by the USCENTCOM commander, SOCCENT forms a JSOTF.

SOCEUR

Special Operations Command Europe headquarters is located at Patch Barracks, Stuttgart, Germany. SOCEUR is a subordinate unified command of U.S. European Command exercising operational control of theater Army, Navy and Air Force Special Operations Forces. SOCEUR is responsible to the commander of USEUCOM and the Supreme Allied Commander Europe for SOF readiness, targeting, exercises, plans, joint and combined training, NATO/partnership activities and execution of counterterrorism, peacetime and contingency operations.

SOCPAC

Special Operations Command Pacific, located at Camp H. M. Smith, Oahu, Hawaii, is a sub-unified command and serves as the SOF component command for the U.S. Pacific Command. The AOR of the commander in chief, USPACOM, represents the largest geographic area of the unified commands. It covers more than half of the Earth's surface with approximately 105 million square miles and nearly 60 percent of the world's population. Distance, diversity, and change characterize the USPACOM AOR.

SOCKOR

Special Operations Command Korea, located at Camp Kim in Yongsan, Korea, is the Theater SOC responsible for Special Operations on the Korean peninsula and, when established, the Korean Theater of Operations. The KTO and SOCKOR exist because there has never been a peace treaty officially ending the Korean War. Military forces on the Korean

Peninsula maintain a heightened state of readiness to respond to the resumption of hostilities with little or no warning.

SOCJFCOM

Special Operations Command - Joint Forces Command is a sub-unified command of USJFCOM and is unique among all other Theater Special Operations Commands assigned to combatant commanders. SOCJFCOM is DOD's primary joint Special Operations Forces trainer and integrator. SOCJFCOM's mission is to train conventional and Special Operations joint force commanders and their staffs in the employment of SOF focusing on full integration of SOF and conventional forces in planning and execution to enhance war-fighting readiness. Located in Norfolk, Va., SOCJFCOM supports all geographic combatant commanders and joint task forces in Overseas Contingency Operations, as well as Combined Joint Special Operations Task Forces in support of Operation Enduring Freedom, Operation Iraqi Freedom, Joint Task Force Horn of Africa, Theater SOCs and the U.S. Special Operations Command Center for Special Operations.

SOCSOUTH

A subordinate unified command of U.S. Southern Command, SOCSOUTH is the theater functional component for Special Operations. It is responsible for all Special Operations Forces in the theater to include civil affairs and military information operations forces. SOCSOUTH's headquarters is located at Homestead Air Reserve Base, Fla. SOCSOUTH is composed of a joint headquarters, three permanently assigned operational units and CONUS-based deployed SOF. The command manages more than 200 SOF deployments per year with an average of 42 missions in 26 countries at any time.

SOCAFRICA

On October 1, 2008, SOCAFRICA was established as U.S. Africa Command's Theater Special Operations Command — a functional, sub-unified special operations command for Africa. SOCAFRICA contributes to U.S. Africa Command's mission through the application of the full spectrum of special operations forces capabilities including civil affairs, information operations, theater security cooperation, crisis response, and campaign planning.

USSOCOM Fact Book

THEATER SPECIAL OPERATIONS COMMANDS

In: U.S. Special Operations Forces
Editor: Michael E. Harris and Roger L. Cook

ISBN: 978-1-61470-507-9
© 2011 Nova Science Publishers, Inc.

Chapter 3

SPECIAL OPERATIONS

Joint Publication 3-05

EXECUTIVE SUMMARY

Commander's Overview

- **Provides an Overview of Joint Special Operations**
- **Describes Special Operations Forces and Their Core Activities**
- **Describes Command and Control of Joint Special Operations**
- **Discusses the Support of Joint Special Operations**

Overview of Special Operations

United States Special Operations Command deploys and sustains special operations forces (SOF) to facilitate operations with conventional forces (CF), to promote synergy among all SOF elements, and to provide more efficient command and control (C2) structures.

Special operations (SO) differ from conventional operations in degree of physical and political risk, operational techniques, modes of employment, and dependence on detailed operational intelligence and indigenous assets. SO are conducted in all environments, but are particularly well suited for denied and politically sensitive environments. SO can be tailored to achieve not only military objectives through application of special operations forces (SOF) capabilities for which there are no broad conventional force requirements, but also to support the application of the diplomatic, informational, and economic instruments of national power.

Special Operations and Their Core Activities

Designated SOF

SOF are those forces identified in Title 10, United States Code (USC), Section 167 or those units or forces that have since been designated as SOF by Secretary of Defense (SecDef). Generally, SOF are under the combatant command (command authority) (COCOM) of the Commander, United States Special Operations Command (CDRUSSOCOM), or the respective geographic combatant commander (GCC) to which they are assigned. SOF are those Active Component and Reserve Component forces of the Services specifically organized, trained, and equipped to conduct and support SO.

Characteristics of SOF

SOF are inherently joint. When employed, SOF are presented with their command and control (C2) structure intact, which facilitates their integration into joint force plans, retains cohesion, and provides a control mechanism to address SO specific concerns and coordinate their activities with other components and supporting commands.

SOF are distinct from conventional forces (CF). Most SOF personnel undergo a careful selection process and mission-specific training beyond basic military skills to achieve entry-level SO skills.

SOF Capabilities. SOF can be formed into versatile, self-contained teams that provide a joint force commander (JFC) with a flexible force capable of operating in ambiguous and swiftly changing scenarios.

SOF are not a substitute for CF. In most cases SOF are neither trained, organized, nor equipped to conduct sustained conventional combat operations and, therefore, should not be substituted for CF that are able to effectively execute that mission.

Most SO missions require non-SOF support.

Five SOF Mission Criteria

It must be an appropriate mission or activity for SOF.
The mission or activities should support the JFC's campaign or operation plan, or special activities.
Mission or tasks must be operationally feasible, approved, and fully coordinated.
Required resources must be available to execute and support the SOF mission.
The expected outcome of the mission must justify the risks.

Special Operations Core Activities

SOF are specifically organized, trained, and equipped to accomplish the 11 core activities: direct action, special reconnaissance, counterproliferation of weapons of mass destruction, counterterrorism, unconventional warfare, foreign internal defense, security force

Special Operations

assistance, counterinsurgency, information operations (IO), military information support operations (MISO), and civil affairs operations.

Command and Control of Special Operations Forces

C2 of SOF normally should be executed within a SOF chain of command.

SOF may be assigned to either CDRUSSOCOM or a GCC. The identification of a C2 organizational structure for SOF should depend upon specific objectives, security requirements, and the operational environment.

Liaison

Liaison among all components of the joint force and SOF, however they are organized, is vital for effective SOF employment, as well as coordination, deconfliction, synchronization, and the prevention of fratricide.

SOF in the United States

Unless otherwise directed by SecDef, all SOF based in the continental United States are assigned to United States Special Operations Command (USSOCOM) and under the COCOM of CDRUSSOCOM. USSOCOM is a unified command (Title 10, USC, Section 167) that has the responsibilities of a functional combatant command and responsibilities similar to a Military Department in areas unique to SO.

SOF in Theater

SOF assigned to a GCC are under the COCOM of the respective GCC. A GCC normally exercises operational control of all assigned and attached SOF through the commander, theater special operations command (CDRTSOC) or a subordinate JFC. The CDRTSOC also may be designated as the joint force special operations component commander (JFSOCC) by the GCC.

Theater Special Operations Command

The theater special operations command (TSOC) is the primary theater SOF organization capable of performing broad continuous missions uniquely suited to SOF capabilities. The TSOC is also the primary mechanism by which a GCC exercises C2 over SOF.

SOF Operational C2

The **JFSOCC** is the commander within a unified command, subordinate unified command, or joint task force (JTF) responsible to the establishing commander for making recommendations on the proper employment of assigned, attached, and/or made available for tasking SOF and assets; planning and coordinating SO; or accomplishing such operational missions as may be assigned. The JFSOCC is given the authority necessary to accomplish missions and tasks assigned.

A **joint special operations task force (JSOTF)** is a JTF composed of SO units from more than one Service, formed to carry out specific SO or prosecute SO in support of a theater campaign or other operations. A JSOTF may have CF tasked to support the conduct of specific missions.

SOF Subordinate C2 Organizations. A JSOTF, by its joint designation, has SOF from more than one of the Services: Army SOF, Navy SOF, Air Force SOF, or Marine Corps SOF, and these designations typically denote their forces and subordinate units, not a headquarters.

SOF as the Lead for a Joint Task Force

Such a construct calls for a SOF joint force commander, not as a joint force special operations component commander/commander joint special operations task force, but as the commander, joint task force.

In some cases, a C2 construct based on *SO expertise and influence* may be better suited to the overall conduct of an operation (i.e., superiority in the aggregate of applicable capabilities, experience, specialized equipment, and knowledge of and relationships with relevant populations), with the JTF being built around a core SO staff. Such a JTF has both SOF and CF and the requisite ability to command and control them. SOF and their unique capabilities are particularly well-suited for such complex situations because of their regional familiarity, language and cultural awareness, and understanding of the social dynamics within and among the relevant populations (i.e., tribal politics, social networks, religious influences, and customs and mores).

Integration and Interoperability of CF and SOF

Effective SOF-CF integration facilitates the synchronizing of military operations in time, space, and purpose; maximizes the capability of the joint force; allows the JFC to optimize the principles of joint operations in planning and execution; and may produce an operating tempo and battle rhythm with which the enemy is unable to cope. It may also reduce the potential for fratricide. Accordingly, focus should be placed on three key areas: operations, command relationships, and liaisons.

Coordination and Liaison Elements

SOF commanders have specific elements that facilitate liaison and coordination. They include the special operations command and control element (SOCCE) to command and control, and coordinate SOF activities with CF; the special operations liaison element (SOLE) to provide liaison to the joint force air component commander (JFACC) or appropriate Service component air C2 facility; and SOF liaison officers placed in a variety of locations as necessary to coordinate, synchronize, and deconflict SO within the operational area.

Joint Special Operations Area

The **JFC may establish a joint special operations area (JSOA),** which is a restricted area of land, sea, and airspace assigned by a JFC to the commander of a joint SO force to conduct SO activities. When a JSOA is designated, the JFSOCC (or commander, joint special operations task force [CDRJSOTF]) is the supported commander within the designated JSOA.

Special Operations

Interorganizational Coordination

Interagency coordination is as integral to SO as it is conventional operations, and fostering personal relationships between SOF commanders and interorganizational leaders and professional relations between both staffs should be a routine objective during military engagement activities.

Multinational Coordination

SOF operate with multinational forces, i.e., forces belonging to a coalition or alliance, on a routine and recurring basis. US SOF assess, train, advise, assist, and operate with a plethora of multinational foreign SO units.

Support Considerations for Special Operations Forces

SOF support must be tailored to specific mission requirements, yet flexible enough to respond to changing employment parameters.

The joint character of SO requires support arrangements across Service lines with emphasis on unique support required in order to sustain independent and remote operations. Further, SOF must be able to exploit information derived from the full range of available multinational, national, theater, and tactical intelligence, surveillance, and reconnaissance support systems.

Intelligence Support

All-source, fused intelligence is vital in identifying relevant targets, course of action development, and mission planning/execution. SO require detailed planning, often by relatively small units. Consequently, intelligence requirements are normally greater in scope and depth than that of CF. Joint intelligence preparation of the operational environment provides the foundation for SO intelligence production.

Operational Contract Support

The continual introduction of high-tech equipment, coupled with force structure and manning limitations, and high operating tempo mean that SOF may be augmented with contracted support, including contingency contractor employees and all tiers of subcontractor employees who are specifically authorized through their contract to accompany the force and have protected status in accordance with international conventions (i.e., contractors authorized to accompany the force).

Host-Nation Support

Host-nation support (HNS) is that civil and/or military assistance rendered by a nation to foreign forces within its territory based on agreements mutually concluded between nations. For SO, HNS must be weighed against operations security considerations, mission requirements and duration, and the operational environment.

Logistic Support

GCCs and their Service component commanders, in coordination with the CDRTSOC, are responsible for ensuring that effective and responsive support systems are developed and provided for assigned/attached SOF.

Health Service Support

SOF teams frequently operate in remote areas and therefore, are exposed to health threats not normally seen in the other areas of the respective host nations. Point-to-point movement to designated Medical Treatment Facilities is standard while medical regulating and strategic aeromedical evacuation might be required and should be part of the contingency planning process.

Communications Systems Support

Communications systems support to SOF normally are global, secure, and jointly interoperable. It must be flexible so that it can be tailored to specific SO missions and it must add value to the SOF operational capability. SOF must be able to communicate anywhere and anytime using the full range of national capabilities required to support the mission.

Public Affairs Support

The diplomatic and political sensitivity of many SO mandates that thorough and accurate public affairs guidance be developed during the operational planning stage and approved for use in advance of most SO.

Combat Camera Support

Combat camera provides still and video documentary products that support MISO and other SO missions. Many combat camera teams supporting SOF are specially equipped with night vision and digital image transmission capabilities.

Legal Support

SO missions frequently involve a unique set of complex issues. There are federal laws and executive orders, federal agency publications and directives, the law of armed conflict, and rules of engagement that may affect SO missions as well as the SO joint planning and targeting processes.

Protection

Protection focuses on conserving the SOF fighting potential, whether operating independently, or as part of a larger joint force in a major operation/campaign. For force protection, typically each GCC has tactical control of US forces in their area of responsibility.

Fire Support

SOF may require long-range, surface-based, joint fire support in remote locations or for targets well beyond the land, maritime, and amphibious operational force area of operations. SOF liaison elements coordinate fire support through both external and SOF channels. SOF liaison elements (e.g., SOCCE and SOLE) provide SOF expertise to coordinate, synchronize, and deconflict SOF fire support.

Special Operations

59

Air Support

In addition to their organic air capabilities for infiltration, exfiltration, resupply, and precision fire support, SOF often require conventional air support that requires timely and detailed planning and coordination. Air support is typically provided by the JFACC (or an Air Force component commander), and the JFSOCC/CDRJSOTF normally provides a SOLE to the JFACC at the joint air operations center.

Maritime Support

Maritime support is provided by the joint force maritime component commander, the Navy component commander, and/or the Marine Corps component commander. Maritime support includes fire support, seabasing operations, deception, and deterrence.

Space Support

Space based support to SOF can include: precision navigation and/or geopositioning, global communications, global intelligence collection, surveillance and warning, meteorological support, imagery for geospatial support and targeting, blue force tracking data, and denying adversary use of space-based capabilities.

Meteorological and Oceanographic Support

This [meteorological and oceanographic support] information can be used by the commander to choose the best windows of opportunity to execute, support, and sustain specific SOF operations.

Cyberspace Support

Cyberspace operations in support of SO can often be conducted remotely, thus reducing the SOF footprint and contributing to freedom of action within a given operational area.

Information Operations Support

IO is a SOF core activity, and also integral to the successful execution of many SO. SO may require support from any combination of core, supporting, or related IO capabilities, so the JFC's IO cell should include a SOF representative.

Multinational Support

Multinational support to SOF complements HNS and depends on mission and capability requirements. Common examples include information and intelligence sharing; providing liaison teams and support to planning efforts; materiel assistance; basing, access, and overflight permission; humanitarian assistance; and linguists and cultural advice and awareness.

Conclusion

This publication provides overarching doctrine for SO and the employment and support of SOF across the range of military operations.

I. OVERVIEW OF SPECIAL OPERATIONS

"Today we see a bewildering diversity of separatist wars, ethnic and religious violence, coups d'état, border pushing waves of poverty-stricken, war-ridden immigrants (and hordes of drug traffickers as well) across national boundaries. In the increasingly wired global economy, many of these seemingly small conflicts trigger strong secondary effects in surrounding (and even distant) countries. Thus a "many small wars" scenario is compelling military planners in many armies to look afresh at what they call "special operations" or "special forces"— the niche warriors of tomorrow."

Alvin and Heidi Toffler
War and Anti-War, Survival at the Dawn of the 21st Century 1993

1. Introduction

This publication provides fundamental principles and guidance for the Services, combatant commanders (CCDRs), and subordinate joint force commanders (JFCs) to prepare for and conduct special operations (SO). It describes those military operations and provides general guidance for military commanders to employ and execute command and control (C2) of special operations forces (SOF) assigned/attached to a geographic combatant commander (GCC), subordinate unified commander, or a commander, joint task force (CJTF). Other specific SO operational guidelines are provided in Joint Publication (JP) 3-05.1, *Joint Special Operations Task Force Operations*; JP 3-13.2, *Military Information Support Operations*, JP 3-22, *Foreign Internal Defense,* and JP 3-57, *Civil-Military Operations*. Additionally, SOF maintain core competencies in counterinsurgency (COIN) and counterterrorism (CT) operations that are discussed in detail in JP 3-24, *Counterinsurgency Operations,* and JP 3-26, *Counterterrorism.* This chapter introduces SO, the nature of SO, and how they relate to the principles of joint operations and the range of military operations. Chapter II, "Special Operations Forces and Their Core Activities," focuses on the SOF and particularly the 11 SOF core activities. Chapter III, "Command and Control of Special Operations Forces," discusses C2 and coordination, and Chapter IV, "Support Considerations for Special Operations Forces," outlines numerous support considerations for SOF.

2. Special Operations

SO are conducted in all environments, but are particularly well suited for denied and politically sensitive environments. SO can be tailored to achieve not only military objectives through application of SOF capabilities for which there are no broad conventional force requirements, but also to support the application of the diplomatic, informational, and economic instruments of national power. SO are typically low visibility or clandestine operations. SO are applicable across the range of military operations. They can be conducted independently or in conjunction with operations of conventional forces (CF) or other government agencies (OGAs), or host nations (HNs)/partner nations (PNs), and may include operations with or through indigenous, insurgent, and/or irregular forces. SO differ from conventional operations in degree of physical and political risk, operational techniques, modes of employment, and dependence on detailed operational intelligence and indigenous assets.

a. SO are often conducted at great distances from major operating bases with operating units widely separated in a distributed manner across the operational area(s). SOF employ sophisticated communications systems and special means of infiltration, support, and exfiltration to penetrate and return from hostile, denied, or politically sensitive areas.

b. SO typically are an integral part of theater campaigns. While SO can be conducted unilaterally in support of specific theater or national objectives, the majority of SO are designed and conducted to enhance the likelihood of success of the overall theater campaign. SO must complement— not compete with nor be a substitute for— conventional operations.

c. The successful conduct of **SO rely on individuals and small units proficient** in specialized skills trained to be applied with adaptability, improvisation, and innovation. While organized for independent operations, SOF effectiveness can often be enhanced when SOF are supported by non-SOF organizations. SO normally require precise tactical-level planning, detailed intelligence, and knowledge of the culture(s) and language(s) of the areas in which the missions are to be conducted. **Rigorous training and mission rehearsals** are integral to the conduct of most SO. SO conducted by small-size SOF units with unique capabilities and self-sufficiency (for short periods of time) provide the United States with additional options for feasible and appropriate military responses. These responses may result in lower degrees of political liability or risk of escalation than are normally associated with employment of larger and more visible CF.

d. **SO can be conducted directly** against an adversary in a single engagement, such as direct action (DA) against critical communication nodes, **or indirectly,** by organizing, training, and supporting insurgent forces through unconventional warfare (UW) against a hostile government or occupying force, or supporting an HN force in support of a friendly government through foreign internal defense (FID) and/or security force assistance (SFA). Other indirect methods include military information support operations (MISO) to influence the adversary military or local civilian populace and civil affairs operations (CAO) to provide essential support to a JFC responsible for civil-military operations (CMO). The results of SO are consistently disproportionate to the size of the units involved.

e. Deployed SOF for some mission profiles will require key CF enablers to maximize their operational effectiveness. These enablers are categorized by battlefield operating systems: maneuver; mobility, countermobility, and survivability; fire support; air defense; intelligence; combat service support; and C2. These CF enablers that enhance SOF capabilities vary by the SOF mission requirements and the SOF disposition in relation to CF (varying in scope from collocation with CF to complete isolation).

3. Special Operations across the Range of Military Operations

a. JP 3-0, *Joint Operations,* states the nature of joint operations requires a JFC to organize and employ joint forces to achieve strategic and operational objectives. Each joint operation (and special operation) has a unique political and strategic context, so the balance and nature of military activities applied will vary according to the unique aspects of the mission and operational environment.

b. Military operations, to include SO, vary in scope, purpose, and combat intensity. A fundamental construct that provides context to the intensity of conflict that may occur during joint military activities is the **range of military operations:** from recurring military engagement, security cooperation, and deterrence activities (typically no conflict to low-intensity conflict), to crisis response and limited contingency operations (low to high), and if necessary, to major operations and campaigns (high intensity) as depicted in Figure I-1.

   (1) Use of SOF and SO, concurrent with CF capabilities in **military engagement, security cooperation, and deterrence** activities help shape the operational environment and keep the day-to-day tensions between nations or groups below the threshold of armed conflict, which serves to maintain US global influence.

   (2) SOF, whether employed independently or complementing CF, participate in many of the missions associated with **crisis response and limited contingencies,** such as CMO, FID, and SFA.

   (3) Individual **major operations and campaigns** often contribute to a larger, long-term effort (e.g., Operation ENDURING FREEDOM). For those large scale efforts, SOF and SO are typically part of the shaping of the operational environment, and may conduct significant activities (e.g., CT and COIN) as part of the campaign or operational effort. The nature of the security environment may require US joint forces, including SOF, to engage in several types of operations simultaneously across the range of military operations. For these missions, commanders synchronize offensive, defensive, and stability operations and activities as necessary to achieve objectives.

c. The commander for any particular operation determines the emphasis to be placed on each type of mission or activity. Although specific types of operations are under the various joint military categories in the range of military operations, each type is not doctrinally fixed and could shift within that range. For example, a COIN operation could escalate from a security cooperation activity into a major operation or campaign.

d. SO can be conducted across the range of military operations at all levels of war and throughout all phases of a campaign or operation. While SO can be applied tactically, commanders and planners should focus SO on strategic and operational objectives and end states to maximize efficiency. Some SO are especially suitable for military engagement without conflict. SO provide options which in appropriate circumstances can prove to be the most viable means of achieving certain objectives. GCCs may leverage the theater special operations command (TSOC) to ensure full integration of SOF capabilities when developing theater plans. SO are most effective during crisis when SOF has had enough time (months to years) to conduct pre-crisis activities, build relationships, and build HN/PN SOF capacity as part of shaping operations

(Phase 0) of theater campaign and contingency plans. Longer term preparations for SO provide options for decision makers in times of crisis that would otherwise not be available. Also, pre-crisis SO preparations may provide situational awareness that permits identification of a potential crisis prior to requiring a US military response, thus allowing a whole-of-government solution be applied to de-escalate the situation by dissuading, deterring, or disrupting the parties involved or through mediation.

(1) **The President designates national objectives** and sanctions the military means to achieve them. In pursuit of those objectives, some SO may be conducted under the direct supervision of the President or Secretary of Defense(SecDef).

(2) **Theater objectives are established by each GCC,** based on national strategic guidance, and are an integral part of a theater campaign plan. The GCC should consider integration of SO into the full range of military operations that supports the theater campaign plan and other theater plans.

(3) **Operational objectives established by subordinate JFCs support theater objectives and lead directly to theater success.** SO provide the JFC with a selective, flexible deterrent option or crisis response capability to achieve operational objectives.

(4) When required to achieve the JFC's objectives, SO may be conducted in support of CFand vice versa .

e. CF and SOF Integration:

(1) Exchange and use of liaison and control elements are critical when CF and SOF conduct operations in the same operational area against the same threat.

(2) A thorough understanding of a unit's integration and interoperability planning.

(3) During mission planning, options should consider how to integrate CF and SOF maneuver elements. Detailed planning and execution coordination is required throughout the process.

(4) Successful integration and interoperability of CF and SOF are dependent upon understanding each other's systems, ions.

f. **Presentation of Special Operations Forces.** United States Special Operations Command (USSOCOM) deploys and sustains SOF to facilitate operations with CF, to promote synergy among all SOF elements, and to provide more efficient C2 structures. For military engagement, security cooperation, and deterrence operations, forward based and distributed C2 nodes under the operational control (OPCON) of the TSOC provide the necessary C2 for assigned and attached SOF. For crisis response, contingency, and major operations and campaigns, SOF may deploy a special operations joint task force (SOJTF) where all SOF report to one SO commander and the packaged force includes all enabling capabilities (organic to SO formations and those Service-provided CF capabilities) required to optimize the effectiveness of the SOJTF. A SOJTF is an operational level organization that may have one or more subordinate joint special operations task forces (JSOTFs).

For a detailed discussion of the range of military operations, including the relationship to the instruments of national power, levels of war, and the categories of joint military activities, see JP 1, Doctrine for the Armed Forces of the United States, *and JP 3-0,* Joint Operations.

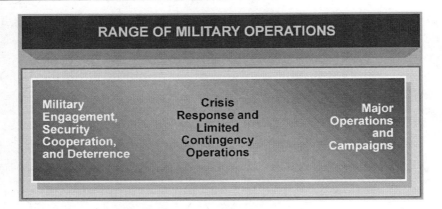

Figure I-1. Range of Military Operations.

II. SPECIAL OPERATIONS FORCES AND THEIR CORE ACTIVITIES

"Special Operations Forces are contributing globally well beyond what their percentage of the total force numbers would indicate. Every day they are fighting our enemies, training and mentoring our partners, and bringing value to tens of thousands of villagers who are still deciding their allegiances."

Admiral Eric T. Olson
Commander, United States Special Operations Command
Statement to the House Armed Services Committee
2 April 2009

1. Introduction

JP 1, *Doctrine for the Armed Forces of the United States,* characterizes traditional warfare (or regular warfare), as a confrontation between nation-states or coalitions/alliances of nation-states involving small to large scale, force-on-force military operations in which adversaries employ a variety of conventional military capabilities against each other in the air, land, maritime, and space physical domains and the information environment (which includes cyberspace). JP 1, *Doctrine for the Armed Forces of the United States,* and JP 3-0, *Joint Operations,* both address irregular warfare (IW) as the pervasive form of warfare of choice by many state adversaries and transnational violent extremists, because of the superiority of the United States in traditional warfare. From the United States perspective, IW encompasses a level of conflict that is less than traditional warfare and involves an adversary seeking to disrupt or negate the military capabilities and advantages of a more powerful, conventionally armed military force, often representing the regime of a nation. However, the strategic objectives of IW are no less significant than those of traditional warfare. Unlike the force-on-force orientation of traditional warfare, IW focuses on the strategic purpose of gaining and maintaining control or influence over, and the support of a relevant population through political, psychological, and economic methods. IW requires a different mindset and different capabilities than those focused on the conventional military defeat of an adversary. The SOF

Special Operations 65

mindset and capabilities make them particularly well suited for all forms of IW. Further, SOF capabilities complement those of CF, whom the Department of Defense (DOD) also has tasked with gaining a core competency in IW. This chapter focuses on who SOF are, their unique characteristics, and the activities they conduct to help attain US strategic objectives.

2. Designated Special Operations Forces

SOF are those forces identified in Title 10, United States Code (USC), Section 167 or those units or forces that have since been designated as SOF by SecDef. Generally, SOF are under the combatant command (command authority) (COCOM) of the commander, United States Special Operations Command (CDRUSSOCOM), or the respective GCC to which they are assigned. SOF are those Active Component and Reserve Component (RC) forces of the Services specifically organized, trained, and equipped to conduct and support SO.

    a.   **US Army.** Special forces (SF), Ranger, Army SO aviation, SO MISO, and SO civil affairs (CA) units.

    b.   **US Navy.** SEAL, SEAL delivery vehicle, and special boat teams.

    c.   **US Air Force.** SO flying units (includes unmanned aircraft systems), special tactics elements (includes combat control, pararescue, SO weather, and select tactical air control party [TACP] units), and aviation FID units.

    d.   **US Marine Corps.** Marine SO battalions which can be task organized to conduct specific SO missions in support of USSOCOM or a supported GCC.

    e.   Certain CF receive enhanced training and/or equipment to support SO and have developed habitual relationships with SOF units to conduct these missions.

3. Characteristics of Special Operations Forces

    a.   **SOF are inherently joint.** SOF regularly conduct joint and combined training, both within the SOF community and with CF. When employed, SOF are presented with their C2 structure intact, which facilitates their integration into joint force plans, retains cohesion, and provides a control mechanism to address SO specific concerns and coordinate their activities with other components and supporting commands. Across the range of military operations, SOF can conduct the broad range of SO including a surgical, rapid, worldwide strike capability. Additionally, SOF routinely operate closely with OGAs, intergovernmental organizations (IGOs), non-governmental organizations (NGOs), and other nations' forces. The complex and sometimes clandestine/low visibility nature of SO and the demanding environments in which such operations are conducted require carefully selected, highly trained and educated, and experienced warriors. SOF require unique training and education, and may also require the development, acquisition, and employment of weapons and equipment not standard for other Armed Forces of the United States.

    b.   **SOF are distinct from CF.** Commanders should be familiar with these characteristics as well as the SOF capabilities and limitations to better select missions and tasks compatible with their capabilities.

(1) Most SOF personnel undergo a careful selection process and mission-specific training beyond basic military skills to achieve entry-level SO skills. These programs make rapid replacement or regeneration of personnel or capabilities unlikely.

(2) SOF organizational structures tend to be populated by mature and seasoned personnel, many of whom maintain high levels of competency in more than one military specialty.

(3) Selected SOF are regionally, culturally, and linguistically oriented for employment; extensive language and cross-cultural training are a routine part of their development.

c. **SOF Capabilities.** SOF can be formed into versatile, self-contained teams that provide a JFC with a flexible force capable of operating in ambiguous and swiftly changing scenarios. They can:

(1) Be task-organized quickly and deployed rapidly to provide tailored responses to many different situations.

(2) Gain access to hostile or denied areas.

(3) Provide limited medical support for themselves and those they support.

(4) Communicate worldwide with organic equipment.

(5) Conduct operations in austere, harsh environments without extensive support.

(6) Survey and assess local situations and report these assessments rapidly.

(7) Work closely with regional military and civilian authorities and populations.

(8) Organize people into working teams to help solve local problems.

(9) Deploy with a generally lower profile and less intrusive presence than CF.

(10) Provide unconventional options for addressing ambiguous situations.

d. **SOF Limitations**

(1) SOF cannot be quickly replaced or reconstituted nor can their capabilities be rapidly expanded. Improper employment of SOF (e.g., in purely conventional roles or on inappropriate or inordinately high-risk missions) runs the risk of rapidly depleting these resources.

(2) **SOF are not a substitute for CF.** In most cases SOF are neither trained, organized, nor equipped to conduct sustained conventional combat operations and, therefore, should not be substituted for CF that are able to effectively execute that mission.

(3) **Most SO missions require non-SOF support.** SOF are typically provided to GCCs and are not structured with robust means of logistic and sustainment capabilities. SOF must rely on the supported GCC's Service component commands for most support except for those SOF-unique assets that are required to be supplied by USSOCOM.

e. **SOF Mission Criteria.** The employment of SOF is facilitated by five basic criteria that provide guidelines for both SOF and CF commanders and planners when considering the employment of SOF (see Figure II-1.)

(1) **It must be an appropriate mission or activity for SOF. SOF should normally be employed against targets with strategic or operational relevance.** SOF should be used to create effects that require SOF's unique skills and capabilities. If the mission or task does not require those skills and capabilities, SOF should not be employed.

Special Operations

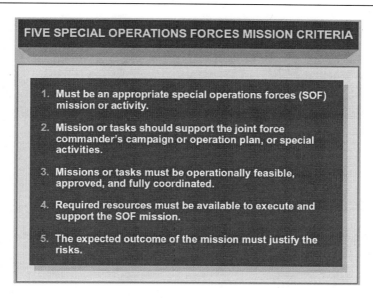

Figure II-1. Five Special Operations Forces Mission Criteria.

    (2) **The mission or activities should support the JFC's campaign or operation plan, or special activities.** If not, shortfall in SOF capabilities should be pointed out and appropriate SOF missions recommended.

    (3) **Mission or tasks must be operationally feasible, approved, and fully coordinated.** SOF are not structured for attrition or force-on-force warfare and should not be assigned missions nor employed beyond their capabilities. For example, during planning and execution JFCs and SOF commanders and their staffs must consider the vulnerability of SOF units to larger, more heavily armed or mobile forces, particularly in a hostile environment. They should also synchronize their operations with those of other components within the operational area and coordinate the timing and location of support requirements with the appropriate commanders.

    (4) **Required resources must be available to execute and support the SOF mission.** Some SOF missions require support from other forces for success, especially for long-term operations, and those operations supporting HNs with limited supporting assets. Such support involves aiding, protecting, complementing, and sustaining the employed SOF, and can include airlift, intelligence, communications, information operations (IO), medical, logistics, space, weather, chemical, biological, radiological, and nuclear (CBRN) defense, and other types of support. Although a target may be vulnerable to SOF, mission support deficiencies may affect the likelihood for success or may entirely invalidate the feasibility of employing SOF.

    (5) **The expected outcome of the mission must justify the risks.** SOF are high-value assets and limited in numbers and resources. Commanders should ensure that the benefits of successful missions are measurable and in balance with the risks in the mission assessment. Risk management analysis should consider not only the potential loss of SOF units and equipment, but also the risk of adverse

effects on US diplomatic and domestic political interests if the mission fails. While the use of SOF may present the potential for a proportionally greater influence on the JFC's campaign or operation, there are some operations that SOF can execute that will make only a marginal contribution while presenting a high risk of personnel and material loss. When contemplating SO, commanders must balance potential SOF losses against the potential operational gain.

4. Special Operations Core Activities

SOF are specifically organized, trained, and equipped to accomplish the 11 core activities listed in Figure II-2. **The core activities represent the collective capabilities of all joint SOF rather than those of any one Service or unit.** While CF also conduct many of these activities (e.g., FID, SFA, COIN, and CT), SOF conduct them using specialized tactics, techniques, and procedures, and to unique conditions and standards in a manner that complement CF capabilities. Use of SOF with CF creates an additional and unique capability to achieve objectives that may not be otherwise attainable. SOF can arrange and package their capabilities in combinations to provide DOD options applicable to a broad range of strategic and operational challenges. Additionally, SOF can perform other activities of a collateral nature such as counterdrug operations and noncombatant evacuation operations. SOF also conduct preparation of the environment as a type of shaping activity supporting core activities that may be conducted in the future.

   a. **Direct Action.** DA entails short-duration strikes and other small-scale offensive actions conducted as SO in hostile, denied, or diplomatically sensitive environments, and which employ specialized military capabilities to seize, destroy, capture, exploit, recover, or damage designated targets. DA differs from conventional offensive actions in the level of diplomatic or political risk, the operational techniques employed, and the degree of discriminate and precise use of force to achieve specific objectives. In the conduct of these operations, SOF may employ raids, ambushes, or other direct assault tactics (including close-quarters combat); emplace mines and other munitions; conduct standoff attacks by fire from air, ground, or maritime platforms; provide terminal guidance for precision-guided munitions; conduct independent sabotage; conduct anti-ship operations, as well as ship boarding and seizure (e.g., maritime interception operations).

   (1) Normally limited in scope and duration, DA usually incorporates an immediate withdrawal from the planned objective area. These operations can provide specific, well-defined, and often time-sensitive results of critical significance at the operational and strategic levels of war.

   (2) SOF may conduct DA independently or as part of larger conventional or unconventional operation or campaign. Although normally considered close combat DA also includes sniping and other standoff attacks by fire delivered or directed by SOF. Standoff attacks are preferred when the target can be damaged or destroyed without close combat. SOF employ close combat tactics and techniques when the mission requires precise or discriminate use of force or the recovery or capture of personnel or materiel.

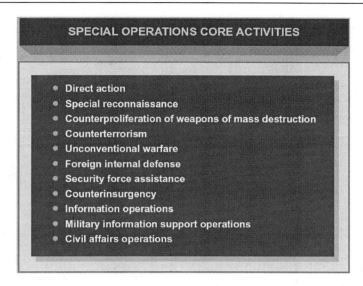

Figure II-2. Special Operations Core Activities.

(3) DA missions may also involve locating, recovering, and restoring to friendly control selected persons or materiel that are isolated and threatened in sensitive, denied, or contested areas. These missions usually result from situations that involve political sensitivity or military criticality of the personnel or materiel being recovered from remote or hostile environments. These situations may arise from a political change, combat action, chance happening, or mechanical mishap. DA usually differs from personnel recovery by the former's use of dedicated ground combat elements, unconventional techniques, precise survivor-related intelligence, and indigenous assistance.

(4) DA, whether unilateral or combined, are short-duration, discrete actions. The SOF command executes DA to achieve the supported commander's objectives.

b. **Special Reconnaissance (SR).** SR entails reconnaissance and surveillance actions conducted as SO in hostile, denied, or diplomatically sensitive environments to collect or verify information of strategic or operational significance, employing military capabilities not normally found in CF. These actions provide an additive collection capability for commanders and supplement other conventional reconnaissance and surveillance actions. SR may include collecting information on activities of an actual or potential enemy or securing data on the meteorological, hydrographic, or geographic characteristics of a particular area. SR may also include assessment of chemical, biological, residual nuclear, radiological, or environmental hazards in a denied area. SR includes target acquisition, area assessment, and post-strike reconnaissance, and may be accomplished by air, land, or maritime assets.

(1) SR complements national and theater intelligence collection assets and systems by obtaining specific, well-defined, and time-sensitive information of strategic or operational significance. SR may also complement other collection methods constrained by weather, terrain-masking, or hostile countermeasures. Selected SOF conduct SR when authorized, to place "eyes on target" in hostile, denied, or diplomatically sensitive territory. SR typically provides essential information to

develop a commander's situational awareness necessary for a command decision, follow-on mission, or critical assessment.

(2) Using SOF for SR enables the JFC to enhance situational awareness and facilitate staff planning and execution of joint operations, whether by CF, SOF, or integrated CF-SOF elements. However, CF-SOF integration does not mean that SOF will become dedicated reconnaissance assets for CF. Rather, the JFC typically tasks SOF through their JSOTF or TSOC to provide SR within a joint special operations area (JSOA), and/or the JFC may task SOF on a case-by-case basis to conduct SR within a CF's operational area.

(3) SOF may also employ advanced reconnaissance and surveillance sensors and collection methods that utilize indigenous assets.

c. **Counterproliferation (CP) of Weapons of Mass Destruction (WMD).** CP refers to actions taken to defeat the threat and/or use of WMD against the United States, our forces, allies, and partners. WMD are chemical, biological, radiological, or nuclear weapons capable of a high order of destruction or causing mass casualties and exclude the means of transporting or propelling the weapon where such means is a separable and divisible part from the weapon. The major objectives of combating WMD policy, which include nonproliferation, CP, and consequence mitigation activities, are to prevent the acquisition of WMD and delivery systems, to stop or roll back proliferation where it has occurred, to deter and defeat the use of WMD and their delivery systems, to adapt US military forces and planning to operate against the threats posed by WMD and their delivery systems, and to mitigate the effects of WMD use. The continued spread of WMD technology can foster regional unrest and provide terrorist organizations with new and potent weapons. SOF provide the following capabilities for this core activity:

(1) Expertise, materiel and teams to supported combatant command teams to locate, tag, and track WMD, as required.

(2) Capabilities to conduct DA in limited access areas, as required.

(3) Build partnership capacity for conducting CP activities.

(4) Conduct IO and MISO to dissuade adversary reliance on WMD.

(5) Other specialized capabilities to combat WMD.

For further information on CP of WMD, refer to JP 3-40, Combating Weapons of Mass Destruction.

d. **Counterterrorism.** Terrorism has evolved over several decades from a tactic of inducing fear in select populations to a transnational threat of strategic proportions, particularly against the United States, Western societies, and emerging democracies perpetuated primarily by groups of violent extremists. Today, whether the extremists are local insurgents or members of an international terrorist network, they are generally viewed as terrorists if they use terrorist tactics. Furthermore, the threat to US interests posed by violent extremists will increase as the continued proliferation of WMD presents an opportunity for terrorists to acquire and use them. CT is a form of IW.

(1) CT is defined as actions taken directly against terrorist networks and indirectly to influence and render global and regional environments inhospitable to terrorist networks. In addition to being a SOF core activity, CT is part of the DOD's broader construct of combating terrorism (CbT), which is actions, including

antiterrorism and CT, taken to oppose terrorism throughout the entire threat continuum.

(2) The United States Government (USG) policy on CbT is to defeat violent extremism and create a global environment that is inhospitable to violent extremists. The broad USG strategy is to continue to lead an international effort to deny violent extremist networks the resources and functions they need to operate and survive. The DOD strategy for CbT implements the following objectives from the *National Strategy for Combating Terrorism*, objectives that are derived from the *National Security Strategy (NSS)*:

(a) Thwart or defeat terrorist attacks against the US, our PNs, and our interests.

(b) Attack and disrupt terrorist networks abroad so as to cause adversaries to be incapable or unwilling to attack the US homeland, allies, or interests.

(c) Deny terrorist networks WMD.

(d) Establish conditions that allow PNs to govern their territory effectively and defeat terrorists.

(e) Deny a hospitable environment to violent extremists.

(3) CDRUSSOCOM is responsible for synchronizing planning for global operations against terrorist networks, in coordination with other combatant commands, the Services and, as directed, appropriate USG agencies.

(4) Success in the global CT effort requires interorganizational coordination to maximize the effectiveness of all the instruments of national power of the United States and PNs. USSOCOM, as the integrating command for global CT planning efforts, supports a global combating terrorism network (GCTN)—a growing network of relationships and liaison partnerships, a supporting technical infrastructure, and the use of information sharing policies. Along with interagency partners, this network draws upon an increasing number of countries, regional organizations, IGOs, NGOs, and the private sector to achieve unified action.

(5) The DOD global campaign plan for the war on terrorism requires integration of both the direct and indirect approaches. The ability to manage both approaches and harness their synergistic effects is vital to the success of both near- and long-term CT objectives, whether within the scope of a theater operation/campaign of a GCC, or the global campaign.

(a) **Direct Approach.** The direct approach consists of actions taken against terrorists and terrorist organizations to disrupt or defeat a specific threat through neutralization or destruction of the network (including individuals, resources, and support structures) and to prevent the reemergence of a threat. This approach may include the use of SOF core activities such as CT, SR, DA, MISO, IO, CAO, and CP.

(b) **Indirect Approach.** The indirect approach consists of the means by which the GCTN can influence the operational environments within which CT operations/campaigns are conducted. This approach usually includes actions taken to enable GCTN partners to conduct operations against terrorists and their organizations as well as actions taken to shape and stabilize their operational environments as a means to erode the capabilities of terrorist organizations and degrade their ability to acquire support and sanctuary. The indirect approach includes use of the SOF core activities such as FID, SFA, IO, MISO, and CAO. These activities combined with stability operations, counterintelligence, CMO, and strategic communication produce synergies to enable partners to combat terrorist organization, deter tacit and active support for terrorism, and erode support for terrorist ideologies.

For further information on CT, refer to JP 3-26, Counterterrorism.

e. **Unconventional Warfare.** UW are those activities conducted to enable a resistance movement or insurgency to coerce, disrupt, or overthrow a government or occupying power by operating through or with an underground, auxiliary, and guerrilla force in a denied area. The United States may engage in UW across the spectrum of armed conflict from major campaigns to limited contingency operations. The US has conducted UW in support of insurgent movements attempting to overthrow an adversarial regime as well as in support of resistance movements to defeat occupying powers (e.g., the Nicaraguan Contras and the Afghan Mujahedeen). UW was also successfully used against the Taliban in the initial stages of Operation ENDURING FREEDOM in Afghanistan. UW can be an effective way of putting indirect and direct pressure on a hostile government or occupying power.

   (1) Military leaders must carefully consider the costs and benefits prior to making a recommendation to engage in UW. Properly coordinated and executed UW may help set conditions for international crisis resolution on terms favorable to the United States or allies without the need for an overt US CF commitment.

   (2) The conduct of UW can have a strategic military-politico utility that can alter the balance of power between sovereign states, and there is potentially significant political risk both at home and abroad. The paramilitary aspect of UW may place DOD in a supporting role to interorganizational partners. The necessity to operate with a varying mix of clandestine/covert means and ways places a premium on operations security (OPSEC) and all-source intelligence. In UW, as in all conflict scenarios, US military forces must closely coordinate their activities with interorganizational partners to enable and safeguard sensitive operations.

   (3) A JFC typically tasks SOF to conduct the military aspect of UW. It will usually require support relationships with some interagency partners and some Service components. A JFC and staff must be able to conduct/support UW operations simultaneously during both traditional warfare and/or IW.

   (4) While each UW mission is unique, US-sponsored UW generally includes seven phases: preparation, initial contact, infiltration, organization, build-up, employment, and transition. These phases may occur concurrently in some situations or may not be required in others. For example, a large established resistance movement may only require initial contact and build up of logistical support to begin UW activities, thereby bypassing the other earlier phases of preparation, infiltration, and organization. The phases also may occur out of sequence, with each receiving varying degrees of emphasis, such as when members of an indigenous irregular force are moved to another country to be trained, organized, and equipped before being infiltrated back into the designated operational area, either with or without US SOF.

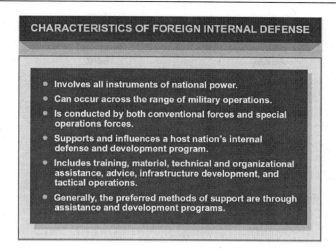

Figure II-3. Characteristics of Foreign Internal Defense.

(5) Senior civilian leaders and JFCs should understand that UW operations require time to mature and reach maximum effectiveness, especially when all of the insurgent or resistance underground networks have to be established.

f. **Foreign Internal Defense.** From the US perspective, FID refers to the US activities that support a HN's internal defense and development (IDAD) strategy designed to protect against subversion, lawlessness, insurgency, terrorism, and other threats to their security, stability, and legitimacy. As shown in Figure II-3, characteristics of FID involve the instruments of national power (diplomatic, informational, military, and economic) through which elements of that power (e.g., financial, intelligence, and law enforcement) can be applied to support a HN's IDAD program. The US FID effort is tailored to the needs of the individual nation or region.

(1) SOF units typically contribute to a FID effort under the OPCON of a TSOC commander, conducting FID operations other than combat, and may require the participating SOF chain of command to have a direct coordination relationship with the chief of mission (COM) or another designee at the appropriate US embassy. In smaller FID operations, SOF units may compose the majority, if not the entire US force. The opposite may be true in a large-scale FID operation, where limits on total troop numbers may result in a smaller number of SOF personnel than CF. In some cases, long-term FID operations may be initiated by SOF, then handed over to CF.

(2) SOF may conduct FID operations unilaterally in the absence of any other military effort, or in support of other ongoing military (i.e., CF) or civilian assistance efforts. FID also supports stability operations designed to promote and protect US national interests by influencing adversarial, political, and information operational variables in a region or country through a combination of peacetime developmental, cooperative activities, and coercive crisis response actions when necessary.

(3) All SOF Service components have capabilities that can contribute to a FID effort. The primary roles of SOF in FID are to assess, train, advise, and assist HN military and paramilitary forces with activities that require the unique

capabilities of SOF. As previously mentioned, SOF may also conduct specialized missions in support of combat operations. The goal is to enable HN forces to maintain the internal stability, to counter subversion and violence in their country, and to address the causes of instability. Each of these key activities plays a role in the accomplishment of the HN IDAD strategy through HN military assistance, population security, and COIN.

(4) FID operations are planned at the national, regional, and especially with SOF units at the local level. FID should involve the integration of all instruments of national power down to the local level. FID operations fall under two major categories—those under the responsibility of DOD and those under the responsibility of the Department of State (DOS) and OGAs. FID has certain aspects that make planning for it complex. Basic imperatives to successfully integrate FID into strategies and plans include the planner having an understanding of US foreign policy; a focus to maintain or increase HN sovereignty and legitimacy; and an understanding of the long-term or strategic implications and sustainability of US assistance efforts. SOF support of FID programs should be tailored to operational, environment, and HN needs. Because FID is a national-level effort involving numerous USG agencies, unity of effort is important.

For further information on FID, refer to JP 3-22, Foreign Internal Defense.

g. **Security Force Assistance.** USG security sector reform (SSR) activities focus on the inextricably linked governmental sectors of security and justice. DOD's primary role in SSR is supporting the reform, restructuring, or reestablishment of the armed forces and the defense sector, which is accomplished through SFA. SFA specifically pertains to those DOD activities that contribute to unified action by the USG to support the development of the capacity and capability of foreign security forces (FSF) and their supporting institutions. FSF include but are not limited to military forces; police forces; border police, coast guard, and customs officials; paramilitary forces; interior and intelligence services; forces peculiar to specific nations, states, tribes, or ethnic groups; prison, correctional, and penal services; and the government ministries or departments responsible for the above services. The US military engages in activities to enhance the capabilities and capacities of a PN (or regional security organization) by providing training, equipment, advice, and assistance to those FSF organized under the equivalent of a national ministry of defense (or an equivalent regional military or paramilitary force), while other USG agencies focus on those FSF assigned to other ministries such as interior, justice, or intelligence services.

(1) USSOCOM is the designated joint proponent for SFA, with responsibility to lead the collaborative development, coordination, and integration of the SFA capability across DOD. This includes development of SFA joint doctrine; training and education for individuals and units; joint capabilities; joint mission essential task lists; and identification of critical individual skills, training, and experience. Additionally, in collaboration with the Joint Staff and United States Joint Forces Command (USJFCOM), and in coordination with the Services and GCCs, USSOCOM is tasked with developing global joint sourcing solutions that recommend the most appropriate forces (CF and/or SOF) for a SFA mission.

Special Operations

(2) SFA includes activities of organizing, training, equipping, rebuilding, and advising various components of FSF. SOF/CF performing SFA conduct initial assessment of the FSF they will assist and then establish a shared way to continue assessing them throughout their development. The HN/PN determines the structure of its military forces, to include approving all organizational designs. These may include changing the numbers of forces, types of units, and internal organizational designs.

(3) Conducting successful SFA operations requires an advisor's mindset and dedication to working through or with FSF. The responsible CCDR tasking US forces to conduct SFA must emphasize that legitimacy is vital for both the US and its partners.

(4) FID and SFA are similar at the tactical level where advisory skills are applicable to both. At operational and strategic levels, both FID and SFA focus on preparing FSF to combat lawlessness, subversion, insurgency, terrorism, and other internal threats to their security; however, SFA also prepares FSF to defend against external threats and to perform as part of an international force. Although FID and SFA are both subsets of security cooperation, neither are considered subsets of the other.

For further information on FID and SFA, refer to JP 3-22, Foreign Internal Defense.

h. **Counterinsurgency.** COIN refers to the comprehensive civilian and military efforts taken to defeat insurgency and to address any core grievances. The combat skills, experience, cultural awareness, and language skills of SOF allow them to conduct a wide array of missions working through or with HN security forces or integrated with US CF, which make them particularly suitable for COIN operations or campaigns.

(1) **Operational Approaches.** There are three primary operational approaches to COIN: direct, indirect, and balanced. The direct approach focuses on protecting US and HN interests while attacking the insurgents. The indirect approach focuses on establishing conditions (a stable and more secure environment) for others to achieve success with the help of the US. The balanced approach is a combination of the direct and indirect methods. **Commanders adjust their approach as circumstances change, but the COIN approach should strive to move from direct to balanced, and ultimately to indirect.** However, the scale of effort for any approach will vary according to operational requirements and overall objectives for the COIN operations or campaign.

(a) **Direct.** A direct approach may be required where an HN government is losing ground in its struggle with an insurgency or there is no viable HN government. The first task in this situation is to establish security and control in as wide an area and extent as possible.

(b) **Indirect.** An indirect approach utilizes more development and diplomatic efforts than military efforts to address the insurgency. This approach is best suited to early intervention but requires that the HN be viable and viewed as legitimate.

(c) **Balanced.** The balanced approach is a more even blend of US diplomatic, developmental, and military efforts. Military efforts are secondary and subordinate to diplomatic and development activities when using this approach.

(2) **SOF Contributions to COIN.** The SOF contribution to COIN is critical through all approaches. Their role as warfighters in the direct approach provide the capabilities for urgent, necessary, and largely lethal activities, often with immediate impact—and to create time for the balanced and indirect approaches. SOF are well suited for the balanced and indirect approaches as combat trainers and advisors as well as warfighters. SOF assistance can increase the capability and capacity of HN specialized or irregular units, which helps mitigate manpower and leadership problems common among HN forces in COIN operations or campaigns. SOF also bring the unique capability to quickly adapt their skills with very little additional training to provide decision makers with a responsive tool to achieve US national objectives while avoiding the large footprint that would accompany CF. CA can provide key development assistance in contested areas. All SOF Service components have capabilities that can contribute to a COIN effort.

(3) **Relationship of Other Core Activities to COIN.** COIN is normally conducted as part of a larger FID program supporting the HN government. SOF can also perform a number of other core activities in support of COIN operations seeking to gain credibility with the relevant population. US applications of MISO and CAO can help reinforce the HN's legitimacy and capabilities and reduce insurgent influence over the population. SFA can range from standing up ministries to improving the organization of the smallest security unit and as such is integral to successful COIN operations. CT can be conducted when terrorism is used in an insurgency. COIN also involves SR and DA operations conducted against insurgents and their bases.

(4) **Defining the Operational Environment.** One of the key contributions of SOF during the preparatory phases of a COIN operation is to help define the operational environment and prepare for the entry of CF and supporting governmental agencies. This is accomplished through assessments, shaping, and intelligence activities, some derived from nontraditional sources. SOF assist in the development of cultural intelligence, measure perceptions and attitudes of the population, gain situational awareness through area reconnaissance, and can operate covertly/clandestinely in areas where CF cannot.

(5) **Center of Gravity.** The typical COIN strategic center of gravity is the indigenous population—thus the need to protect the population and gain and maintain popular support. When conducting operations, US forces adhere to the principle of measured and precise use of force—employing proportionality and discrimination. SOF, by their training, regional familiarity, cultural awareness, and understanding of social dynamics within relevant populations focus on establishing cooperative relationships with indigenous populations and with HN security forces to enhance the legitimacy of the government with the population in accordance with the HN IDAD plan.

For more information on COIN, refer to JP 3-24, Counterinsurgency Operations.

i. **Information Operations.** IO are the integrated employment, during military operations, of information-related capabilities in concert with other lines of operation to influence, disrupt, corrupt, or usurp the decision making of adversaries and potential adversaries while protecting our own. When properly coordinated, integrated, and synchronized as a part of the overall operation, IO affect the quality, content, and availability of information available to decision makers. IO also influence the perceptions and motivations of targeted key audiences with the goal of convincing them to act in a manner conducive to established objectives and desired end states. IO are conducted throughout all operational phases, across the range of military operations, and at every level of war.

(1) IO play a key role in the successful accomplishment of SO missions and promote other SOF core activities. For example, electronic warfare (EW) and computer network operations (CNO) disrupt adversary communications and networks while protecting our own fundamental conditions for successful SO missions. Similarly, OPSEC denies the adversary information needed to correctly assess SOF capabilities and intentions. MISO, a vital component of IO and a key SOF activity, can be employed to optimize the psychological impacts (positive or negative) of other SO activities (e.g., CT or COIN) on a variety of target audiences (TAs) and undermine an adversary's will to fight. Military deception (MILDEC) deliberately misleads adversary decision makers as to friendly military capabilities, intentions, and operations. When interwoven with EW and CNO, MILDEC can drive an adversary to take specific actions (or not take action), ultimately contributing to the efficacy of SOF activities (e.g., DA).

(2) In a similar fashion, other SOF activities complement IO and provide assistance toward the accomplishment of strategic and operational IO-related objectives. For example, SR and DA may identify, observe, target, disrupt, capture, or destroy specific capabilities tied to an adversary's C2 (i.e., decision making) processes. Further, successful FID, UW, COIN, and SFA can have a significant psychological impact on an adversary's morale or deliver a detrimental blow to the adversary's ability to recruit and finance operations. SOF may also play a key role in MILDEC by replicating the tactical impact of a much larger force presence.

(3) SOF leaders and staffs must integrate IO throughout all phases of an operation to protect critical capabilities and information, reduce overall risk to the mission and forces, and increase the prospect of mission success. The role of the IO planner is to coordinate, integrate, deconflict, and synchronize IO, and the supporting and related capabilities, whether CF- or SOF-provided, in accordance with the commander's objectives and selected courses of action (COAs). Likewise, the IO cell within the SOF headquarters (HQ) performs the critical function of optimizing the combined effects of SO activities and IO within the information environment; as related to stated SOF objectives, as well as larger operational and strategic end states.

(4) USSOCOM plays a broader, integrating role for IO in support of SOF across the combatant commands. As directed by the Unified Command Plan, USSOCOM integrates and coordinates DOD MISO capabilities to enhance interoperability, and supports United States Strategic Command (USSTRATCOM) with its IO responsibilities and other CCDRs with MISO planning and execution. Additionally, USSOCOM supports the strategic and operational planning,

oversight, and execution of IO and provides IO functional expertise and leadership by assisting in the development of policy, doctrine, future force plans, as well as conducting oversight/coordination of IO requirements for SOF. This includes development, education, joint IO training, experimentation, and advanced technology initiatives.

For further information on IO, refer to JP 3-13, Information Operations.

j. **Military Information Support Operations.** MISO are planned operations to convey selected information and indicators to foreign audiences to influence their emotions, motives, objective reasoning, and ultimately the behavior of foreign governments, organizations, groups, and individuals. The purpose of MISO is to induce or reinforce foreign attitudes and behavior favorable to the originator's objectives.

(1) MISO should be integrated during all phases of operations/campaigns, with both SOF and CF. Effective MISO require the commander's emphasis and active involvement. SO MISO forces and staff planners support the commander by integrating MISO throughout the operation. MISO are executed within carefully reviewed and approved programs and under mission-tailored approval guidelines that flow from national-level authorities.

(2) MISO planners follow a deliberate but responsive process that aligns commander's objectives with a thorough analysis of the environment; select relevant TAs; develop focused, culturally and environmentally tuned messages and actions; employ sophisticated media delivery means and produce observable, measurable behavioral response. However, MISO is most successful when fully synchronized and integrated with complementary actions by the larger joint force and other USG capabilities. The US military message must be congruent with US military actions if TAs are to be persuaded by MISO to modify short-term attitudes and perceptions and long-term behavior.

(3) Effective MISO are continuously planned and conducted across the range of military operations and throughout all phases of operations. In peacetime and limited crises response operations, MISO forces and activities are usually planned and coordinated through the TSOC. In permissive or uncertain environments not involving combat operations, MISO activities are planned and integrated with other operations and with other USG efforts to further national defense strategies through the GCC's theater campaign plan. In major contingencies, the JFC may establish a separate JSOTF known as the joint military information support operations task force (JMISOTF) to conduct MISO.

(4) MISO may be employed within the US under limited circumstances. During natural disasters or national security crises, MISO forces may deploy civil authority information support elements (CAISEs) supporting the designated lead federal agency to support civil authorities. SOF and CF MISO specialists, as part of CAISEs, may provide MISO for civil support (i.e., defense support of civil authorities) following natural disasters or other major crises.

(a) When authorized for employment in this manner, MISO forces inform rather than influence by utilizing their media development, production, and dissemination capabilities to deliver administrative and command information to populations in the operational area. Messages typically include information such as the location of relief sites, how to obtain essential services, disease prevention tips, current civil authority instructions, and similar messages. MISO dissemination assets such as radio broadcast systems, print production, and loudspeaker teams also can augment civilian commercial broadcast capabilities.

(b) All CAISE efforts are coordinated with ongoing military and lead federal agency public affairs (PA) activities as required.

(5) MISO play a key role in SO and in relation to each of the other SOF core activities; particularly in irregular conflicts that focus on ideological and social-political dimensions such as FID, COIN, CT, and UW. For example, MISO military information support teams may deploy to support approved COIN operations, demining, or foreign humanitarian assistance programs under either JFC or US diplomatic control. MISO staff planners and supporting MISO units provide the detailed planning and execution to reduce operational risk, enlist the aid of key populations, and optimize the impact of SO on the achievement of command objectives and USG policy.

(6) USSOCOM retains the preponderance of active duty MISO forces under United States Army Special Operations Command. USSOCOM also gains Air RC MISO forces through Air Force Special Operations Command when those Air National Guard assets are mobilized. To provide a strategic level MISO capability, USSOCOM established the Joint Military Information Support Command (JMISC), a joint subordinate command to serve as a key contributor in DOD's ongoing efforts to erode adversary power, will, and influence. JMISC plans, coordinates, integrates, and manages the execution of transregional information programs to achieve operational, strategic, and national goals and objectives. USSOCOM is the designated DOD proponent for MISO with the responsibility of coordinating the collaborative development and integration of DOD MISO.

For further information on MISO, refer to JP 3-13.2, Military Information Support Operations.

k. **Civil Affairs Operations.** CAO are operations conducted by CA forces that enhance the relationship between military forces and civil authorities in localities where military forces are present. This requires coordination with OGAs, IGOs, NGOs, indigenous populations and institutions, and the private sector. It involves application of CA functional specialty skills that are normally the responsibility of civil government to enhance planned CMO. All CMO must be synchronized and support the commander's intent and operational concept. All CA core tasks support the JFC's CMO objectives.

(1) CAO performed in support of SO are characterized by actions conducted by small CA teams or elements generally without the support of larger military formations, in isolated, austere, and in many cases politically-sensitive environments. Such CAO are unique and require flexibility and ingenuity from CA teams. Successful employment requires planning and support from the CA staff at the supported TSOC. Additionally, these operations require a greater level of planning and coordination with multiple civilian and military partners for decentralized execution.

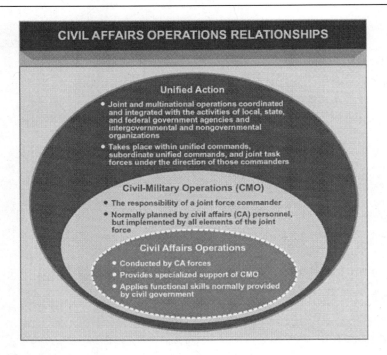

Figure II-4. Civil Affairs Operations Relationships.

(2) CA personnel, leaders, and forces receive advanced skills training specific to CAO. CA teams are trained to identify critical (civil) vulnerabilities, conduct civil reconnaissance, engage HN and interagency counterparts, create country or region specific supporting plans, develop a series of activities to ensure unity of effort to achieve JFC and TSOC objectives, oversee projects, and eventually close activities and actions with assessments and targeting refinement. CA team members should be organized, trained, and prepared to serve as the senior SOF representative in countries with a limited SOF footprint. Figure II-4 depicts the relationship of CAO to overall unified action.

(3) CAO consist of those actions taken to coordinate with HN military and civilian agencies, OGAs, NGOs, or IGOs, in order to support US policy or the military commander's assigned mission. CA core tasks include:
   (a) Populace and resources control,
   (b) Foreign humanitarian assistance,
   (c) Nation assistance,
   (d) Support to civil administrations, and
   (e) Civil information management.

(4) CAO are conducted by CA forces organized, trained, and equipped to provide specialized support to commanders conducting CMO. Commanders having responsibility for an operational area typically will also have responsibility for the civilian populace therein. Commanders conduct CMO to establish, maintain, influence, or exploit relations between military forces and civilian authorities (governmental and nongovernmental) and the civilian populace in a permissive or hostile operational environment to facilitate military operations and to

Special Operations   81

consolidate operational objectives. CA forces may assist in performance of activities and functions by military forces that are normally the responsibility of local government. CMO may be conducted before or during military operations and especially during stability operations.

For further information on CAO, refer to JP 3-57, Civil-Military Operations.

III. COMMAND AND CONTROL OF SPECIAL OPERATIONS FORCES

"If officers desire to have control over their commands, they must remain habitually with them, industriously attend to their instruction and comfort, and in battle lead them well."

General Thomas Jonathan "Stonewall" Jackson
Letter of Instruction to Commanding Officers
Winchester, Virginia, 1861

1. Introduction

a. Command is the most important function undertaken by a JFC as it is the exercise of authority and direction by a properly designated commander over assigned and attached forces. C2 is the means by which a JFC synchronizes and/or integrates joint force activities to achieve unity of command, ties together all the operational functions and activities, and applies to all levels of war and echelons of command across the range of military operations. Effective C2 is a force multiplier that allows commanders to employ their forces toward a common effort. C2 should have a feedback process, or reciprocal influence, that allows commanders to best adapt to rapidly changing circumstances.

b. **SOF may be assigned to either CDRUSSOCOM or a GCC.** C2 of SOF normally should be executed within a SOF chain of command. The identification of a C2 organizational structure for SOF should depend upon specific objectives, security requirements, and the operational environment. Command relationships should be fashioned to provide the necessary guidance given an uncertain, noncontiguous, and asymmetric operational environment without unnecessarily restricting the initiative and flexibility of subordinate commanders. In all cases, commanders exercising command authority over SOF should:

(1) Provide for a clear and unambiguous chain of command.

(2) Avoid frequent transfer of SOF between commanders.

(3) Provide for sufficient staff experience and expertise to plan, conduct, and support the operations.

(4) Integrate SOF earlyin the planning process.

(5) Match unit capabilities with mission requirements.

c. **SOF are most effective when SO are fully integrated into the overall plan.** The ability of SOF to operate unilaterally, independently as part of the overall plan, or in support of a conventional commander requires a robust C2 structure for integration and coordination of the SOF effort. Successful SO require centralized, responsive, and unambiguous C2 through an appropriate SOF C2 element. The limited window of opportunity and sensitive nature of many SOF missions requires a C2 structure that is, above all, responsive to the needs of the operational unit and provides the most flexibility and agility in the application of SOF. SOF C2 may be tailored for a specific mission or operation.

d. **Liaison** among all components of the joint force and SOF, however they are organized, is vital for effective SOF employment, as well as coordination, deconfliction, synchronization, and the prevention of fratricide.

2. Assignment of Special Operations Forces

a. **SOF in the United States.** Unless otherwise directed by SecDef, all SOF based in the continental United States are assigned to USSOCOM and under the COCOM of CDRUSSOCOM. USSOCOM is a unified command (Title 10, USC, Section 167) that has the responsibilities of a functional combatant command and responsibilities similar to a Military Department in areas unique to SO. When directed as a supported commander by the President or SecDef, CDRUSSOCOM plans and conducts certain SO missions worldwide, in coordination with the applicable GCCs.

(1) In its role as a functional combatant command and when directed, USSOCOM provides US-based SOF on a temporary basis to other GCCs for operational employment. When transferred, the forces are **attached** to the gaining combatant command with the GCC normally exercising OPCON over them.

(2) When directed by the President or SecDef, CDRUSSOCOM can establish and employ task forces as a supported commander.

b. **SOF in Theater**

(1) The Armed Forces are predominantly CF and tend to operate as an integrated joint team across the range of military operations using a C2 structure centered on the JFC's mission and concept of operations, available forces and staff capabilities, location, and facilities. The JFC is typically a CF commander, and C2 is guided by principles of simplicity, span of control, unit integrity, and interoperability. This classic C2 framework is based on the *preponderance of forces* and the capability to control them.

(2) SOF assigned to a GCC are under the COCOM of the respective GCC. A GCC normally exercises OPCON of all assigned and attached SOF through the commander, theater special operations command (CDRTSOC) or a subordinate JFC. The CDRTSOC also may be designated as the joint force special operations component commander (JFSOCC) by the GCC (see Figure III-1). TSOCs and their subordinate SOF organizations and C2 coordination and liaison elements ensure that SO are responsive to the needs of the supported JFC, whether the JFC is a GCC or a CJTF.

(3) When a GCC establishes and employs multiple joint task forces (JTFs) and independent task forces, the TSOC commander may establish and employ multiple JSOTFs to manage SOF assets and accommodate JTF/task force SO requirements. Accordingly, the GCC, as the common superior commander,

Special Operations 83

normally will establish supporting or tactical control (TACON) command relationships between JSOTF commanders and JTF/task force commanders.

c. **SOF under control of a non-US command.** When directed by the President or SecDef through the Chairman of the Joint Chiefs of Staff, GCCs may place SOF units under the control of a non-US multinational force commander. In such instances, OPCON of US SOF units will be retained by a US SOF commander within the multinational command structure.

3. Command and Control of Special Operations Forces in Theater

C2 of SOF normally should be executed within a SOF chain of command. C2 of MISO and CA forces will usually be through the SOF chain of command unless the force has been attached to a CF for a specific period or to perform a specific function. The identification of a C2 organizational structure for SOF should depend upon specific objectives, security requirements, and the operational environment. C2 of SOF is executed through one or more of the following:

a. **Theater Special Operations Command.** To provide the necessary unity of command, each GCC (except Commander, US Northern Command) has established a TSOC as a subunified command within their geographic combatant command. US Northern Command maintains an SO division within its operations directorate that serves as a theater SO advisor to the commander. The TSOC is the primary theater SOF organization capable of performing broad continuous missions uniquely suited to SOF capabilities. The TSOC is also the primary mechanism by which a GCC exercises C2 over SOF. The TSOC commander has three principal roles.

(1) **Joint Force Commander.** As the commander of a subunified command, the CDRTSOC is a JFC. As such, he has the authority to plan and conduct joint operations as directed by the GCC and exercises OPCON of assigned commands and forces and normally over attached forces as well. The CDRTSOC may establish JTFs that report directly to him, such as a JSOTF, joint civil-military operations task force (JCMOTF), or JMISOTF, in order to plan and execute these missions.

(2) **Theater SO Advisor.** The CDRTSOC **advises** the GCC, Service component commanders, and designated functional component commanders on the **proper employment of SOF.** The CDRTSOC may develop specific recommendations for the assignment of SOF in theater and opportunities for SOF to support the overall theater campaign plan. The role of theater SO advisor is best accomplished when the GCC establishes the CDRTSOC as a special staff officer on the theater staff (in addition to his duties as a commander— i.e., "dual hatted"). In this case, the CDRTSOC may appoint a deputy as his representative to the theater staff for routine day-to-day staff matters.

(3) **Joint Force Special Operations Component Commander.** When designated by the GCC, the CDRTSOC will function as a JFSOCC. This will normally be the case when the GCC establishes functional component commanders for operations, absent the establishment of a JTF. The CDRTSOC can also be

designated the JFSOCC within a JTF if the scope of the operations warrant it (see Figure III-2).

b. Within a GCC's area of responsibility (AOR), there may be several different command relationships regarding SOF. The JFC who is the establishing authority must designate appropriate command relationships among the SOF commanders, CJTFs, and Service and functional component commanders.

(1) The GCC may directly exercise OPCON over one or more JSOTF.

(2) Typically, a GCC will designate a CDRTSOC or a JFSOCC to exercise OPCON over one or more JSOTFs.

(3) A JFC, subordinate to the GCC (i.e., a CJTF), may have one or more JSOTFs. In this case the JFC would exercise OPCON through a commander, joint special operations task force (CDRJSOTF) or may establish/designate a JFSOCC to exercise OPCON over multiple JSOTFs.

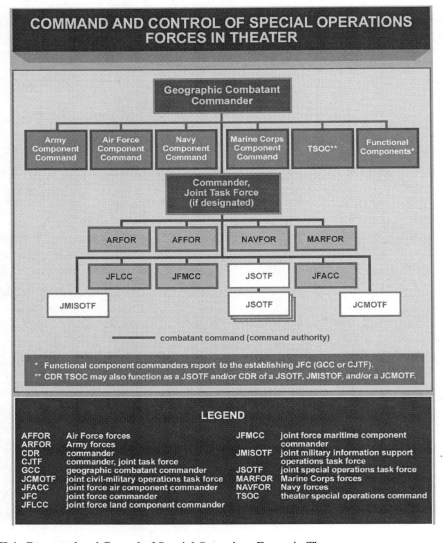

Figure III-1. Command and Control of Special Operations Forces in Theater.

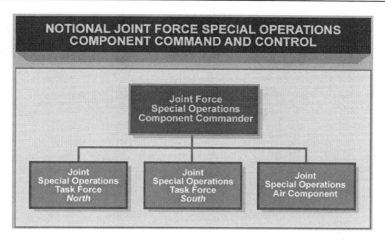

Figure III-2. Notional Joint Force Special Operations Component Command and Control.

(4) A CDRJSOTF may exercise OPCON over subordinate special operations task forces (SOTFs), and a CDRJSOTF typically exercises OPCON over their assigned SOF and OPCON or TACON of attached SOF.

(5) For the purpose of a C2 discussion a JMISOTF and a JCMOTF should be considered in the same context as a JSOTF for establishing command relationships. However, JMISOTFs and JCMOTFs may include both SOF units and CF units which should be a consideration for the JFC when establishing command relationships.

See JP 3-57, Joint Civil-Military Operations, *for additional details regarding CA, JCMOTFs, and CMO, and JP 3-13.2,* Military Information Support Operations, *for additional details regarding JMISOTFs.*

c. **SOF Operational C2**

(1) **JFSOCC.** The JFSOCC is the commander within a unified command, subordinate unified command, or JTF responsible to the establishing commander for making recommendations on the proper employment of assigned, attached, and/or made available for tasking SOF and assets; planning and coordinating SO; or accomplishing such operational missions as may be assigned. The JFSOCC is given the authority necessary to accomplish missions and tasks assigned by the establishing commander (i.e., a GCC or CJTF). The CDRTSOC or a CDRJSOTF will normally be the individual functioning as the JFSOCC. When acting as a JFSOCC, they retain their authority and responsibilities as JFCs. A JFSOCC may have OPCON over one or more JSOTFs. The CDRTSOC will normally be established as a JFSOCC if there is more than one JSOTF to command (see Figure III-2). If only one JSOTF is established (i.e., within a JTF), the CDRJSOTF could also be designated as the JFSOCC by the establishing JFC. When a joint force special operations component (JFSOC) is established and combined with elements from one or more foreign nations, it becomes a combined forces special operations component (SOC), and its commander becomes a combined forces SOC commander, who would likely control or manage employment of those elements in unified action.

(2) **JSOTF.** A JSOTF is a JTF composed of SO units from more than one Service, formed to carry out a specific SO or prosecute SO in support of a theater campaign or other operations. A JSOTF may have CF tasked to support the conduct of specific missions.

(a) A JSOTF, like any JTF, is normally established by a JFC (e.g., a GCC, a subordinate unified commander such as a CDRTSOC, or a CJTF). For example, a GCC could establish a JTF to conduct operations in a specific joint operations area of the theater. Then either the GCC or the CJTF could establish a JSOTF, subordinate to that JTF, to plan and execute SO. Likewise, a CDRTSOC could establish a JSOTF to focus on a specific mission or operational area assigned by the GCC. A JSOTF may also be established as a joint organization and deployed as an entity from outside the theater, in coordination with that GCC.

(b) A JSOTF is established to conduct operations in a specific operational area or to accomplish a specific mission. If geographically oriented, multiple JSOTFs will normally be assigned different operational areas (e.g., separate JSOAs).

(c) When a JSOTF is formed to directly support a GCC, the CDRTSOC normally acts as the CDRJSOTF. Regardless of whom it is, a CDRJSOTF is a JFC and exercises the authority and responsibility assigned by the establishing authority. A JSOTF staff is normally drawn from the TSOC staff or an existing O-6 level HQ from an existing SOF component with augmentation from other SOF or conventional units and/or personnel as appropriate.

(d) When a JSOTF is established and combined with elements from one or more foreign countries, it typically becomes a combined JSOTF and its commander becomes a combined CDRJSOTF.

For further detailed information on a JSOTF, refer to JP 3-05.1, Joint Special Operations Task Force Operations.

d. **SOF Subordinate C2 Organizations.** A JSOTF, by its joint designation, has SOF from more than one of the Services: Army special operations forces (ARSOF), Navy special operations forces (NAVSOF), Air Force special operations forces (AFSOF), or Marine Corps special operations forces (MARSOF), and these designations typically denote their forces and subordinate units, not an HQ. In the context of generic Service SOC HQ, they are the Army special operations component (ARSOC), Navy special operations component (NAVSOC), the Air Force special operations component (AFSOC), and the Marine Corps special operations command (MARSOC), respectively. Normally, the only SOF functional component under a CDRTSOC/JFSOCC/CDRJSOTF is a joint special operations air component (JSOAC). A notional depiction of a JSOAC under a JFSOCC is shown in Figure III-2, and a notional depiction of JSOTF elements (including a JSOAC) is shown in Figure III-3.

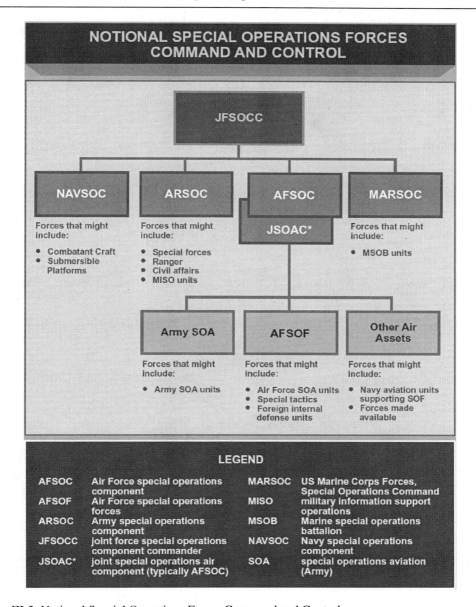

Figure III-3. Notional Special Operations Forces Command and Control.

(1) **ARSOF.** The ARSOC, as the Army Service force component of a JSOTF, is usually designated as a SOTF and consists of one or more of the following forces: SF, Rangers, and Army special operations aviation (Army SOA). The SOTF is normally commanded and manned by an SF or a Ranger battalion commander and staff. The SOTF normally has MISO and CA forces if they are not part of a separate JMISOTF or JCMOTF, respectively.

   (a) **SOTF.** If there is an SF group or SF battalion, or the Ranger Regiment in the tasked ARSOF, it may be designated a SOTF. The CDRJSOTF may establish multiple subordinate SOTFs, with each SOTF organized around the nucleus of an SF or Ranger unit and may include a mix of ARSOF units and their support elements. The CDRJSOTF may assign each SOTF an area within the JSOA or a functional mission.

(b) **Special Forces.** SF units are task-organized as SF groups and battalions, both of which have organic HQ and support elements. When deployed, an SF group or battalion may be designated a SOTF.

(c) **Rangers.** The C2 of Rangers normally is exercised through command posts collocated with other SOF or conventional units. They do not have the organic capability to establish their own forward operations bases. If the Ranger Regiment is deployed, it will normally form a SOTF.

(d) **Army SOA.** The Army SOA are organic ARSOF assets with OPCON normally exercised by the CDRJSOTF through either the Service component, ARSOC, commander, or a joint special operations air component commander (JSOACC), depending on the situation. For example, when a JSOACC is established as a functional component commander by the CDRTSOC/JFSOCC/CDRJSOTF, the Army SOA may be under TACON, or tasked in support of the JSOACC.

(2) **NAVSOF.** The NAVSOC task organization is based on operational requirements. The NAVSOC may include SEALs, submersible platforms, combatant craft, and supporting forces.

(a) Naval Special Warfare Task Force. For a major operation or campaign, the NAVSOC is referred to as a naval special warfare task force (NSWTF) and is commanded by a SEAL captain (O-6). An NSWTF has one or more subordinate naval special warfare task groups (NSWTGs).

(b) NSWTG. The NAVSOC may be an NSWTG commanded by a SEAL commander (O-5). An NSWTG has one or more subordinate naval special warfare task units (NSWTUs).

(3) **AFSOF.** The AFSOC (not to be confused with the Air Force Special Operations Command that is the Air Force component of USSOCOM) is the Air Force component, normally composed of a special operations wing, special operations group, or squadron, and an element of an Air Force special tactics group. A JSOACC, if designated by the JFSOCC/CDRJSOTF, is typically the AFSOC commander. When subordinate AFSOF units deploy to forward operations bases or advanced operations bases, the AFSOC commander may establish one or more provisional units as follows:

(a) **Air Force Special Operations Detachment (AFSOD).** The AFSOD is a squadron-size AFSOF HQ that could be a composite organization composed of different US Air Force assets. The AFSOD normally is subordinate to an AFSOC, JSOAC, JSOTF, or a JTF depending upon the size and duration of the operation, and the joint organizational structure.

(b) **Air Force Special Operations Element (AFSOE).** The AFSOE contains selected AFSOF units that are normally subordinate to an AFSOC or AFSOD.

(4) **MARSOF.** MARSOC is the Marine Corps Service component of USSOCOM. Although MARSOC HQ is nondeployable, when tasked by CDRUSSOCOM, MARSOC units deploy as needed in support of USSOCOM to form, deploy, and

employ a JSOTF. The MARSOFof a JSOTF may be one of the following subordinate commands.

    (a) **Marine SO Battalions.** There are three Marine SO line battalions, each with four companies. These companies can be task organized to conduct SR, DA, SFA, and FID missions in support of USSOCOM or a supported GCC, whether under a CDRJSOTF or a CJTF. These companies may also provide tailored military combat skills training and advisor support for identified foreign forces.

    (b) **Marine SO Support Group.** It provides specified support capabilities for SO missions as directed by the MARSOC.

(5) **JSOAC.** JSOAC collectively refers to the commander, staff, and assets of a SO functional air component of a subordinate unified command, a JFSOC or a JSOTF. A CDRTSOC/JFSOCC/CDRJSOTF may designate a JSOACC to be responsible for the centralized planning and direction and the execution of joint SO air activities, and for coordinating conventional air support for the SOF with the JFC'sjoint force air component commander (JFACC). The JSOACC will normally be the commander with the preponderance of air assets and/or the greatest ability to plan, coordinate, allocate, task, control, and support the assigned/supporting air assets. There may be circumstances when the SOF commander may elect to place selected SO aviation assets under separate control. A JSOACC may be subordinate to a single CDRJSOTF or tasked to support multiple CDRJSOTFs within a JFSOC (see Figure III-2). A JSOAC may be a standing organization or can be formed in response to a contingency or other operation.

4. Special Operations Forces as the Lead for a Joint Task Force

With the increased IW nature of operations and a whole-of-government effort in unified action to defeat global, networked, and transnational irregular adversaries, there may be cases where the C2 construct based on *preponderance of forces* may not be the primary consideration in establishing a JTF. In some cases, a C2 construct based on *SO expertise and influence* may be better suited to the overall conduct of an operation (i.e., superiority in the aggregate of applicable capabilities, experience, specialized equipment, and knowledge of and relationships with relevant populations), with the JTF being built around a core SO staff. Such a JTF has both SOF and CF and the requisite ability to command and control them. SOF and their unique capabilities are particularly well-suited for such complex situations because of their regional familiarity, language and cultural awareness, and understanding of the social dynamics within and among the relevant populations (i.e., tribal politics, social networks, religious influences, and customs and mores). SOF also maintain special relationships with other participants within unified action. Given the SOF expertise and the special operations form of "maneuver," SOF may be best suited to lead US forces in some operational areas. Accordingly, an optimal construct can be one having a SOF chain of command supported by CF and their enabling functions. **Such a construct calls for a SOF JFC, not as a JFSOCC/CDRJSOTF, but as the CJTF.**

a. **TSOC-Based JTF.** An example of this C2 construct is a JTF staff built around a TSOC, integrating SOF and CF with appropriate enabling functions. If needed, the TSOC can be enhanced by a deployable joint task force augmentation cell (DJTFAC). CDRUSSOCOM maintains a DJTFAC, currently identified as *JTF Sword*— a joint, multi-disciplined group of SO planners and staff experts capable of establishing a SOF C2 element or integrating with a forming or formed SOF HQ to rapidly establish a JTF HQ providing C2 for conducting operations within IW. USSOCOM also has a robust global reach-back capability for additional SOF, staff expertise, and special operations-peculiar (SO-peculiar) support. SO-peculiar support is explained in Chapter IV, "Support Considerations for Special Operations Forces."

b. **USSOCOM JTF.** Another example is a unique JTF resourced by and under the C2 of CDRUSSOCOM. The USSOCOM JTF, currently identified as *JTF 487,* is a separately established, deployable, scalable, senior-level HQ that can take command of a complex "direct-indirect" force structure in ambiguous conflict environments to conduct operations within IW. This JTF is not built around a TSOC, nor does it compete with an Army corps or TSOC; however, it can integrate with an established HQ, and can augment a TSOC or other deployed organization. Additionally, the USSOCOM JTF provides a minimal footprint and streamlined leadership hierarchy, using the USSOCOM Global Mission Support Center— a single point of entry providing SOF customers a reach-back, push-forward, and think-ahead capability for operational and emerging requirements.

5. Integration and Interoperability of Conventional Forces and Special Operations Forces

SOF and CF often share the same operational environment for extended periods. While SOF-CF integration poses challenges, there are also great opportunities the JFC may exploit. This integration often creates additional options for achieving objectives. Integration and interoperability enable the JFC to take advantage of both SOF and CF core competencies and Service or SOF unique systems. Effective SOF-CF integration facilitates the synchronizing of military operations in time, space, and purpose; maximizes the capability of the joint force; allows the JFC to optimize the principles of joint operations in planning and execution; and may produce an operating tempo and battle rhythm with which the enemy is unable to cope. It may also reduce the potential for fratricide. Accordingly, focus should be placed on three key areas: operations, command relationships, and liaisons.

a. **Operations**
   (1) As CF now perform some traditional SOF roles, such as providing advisor teams to FSF, it is especially important that SOF and CF start planning and integrating operations, beginning with the first efforts at mission development and concluding with the achievement of the desired end state.
   (2) SOF and CF units should integrate early, prior to deployments, to build and foster relationships, understand each others' misconceptions or friction points. When possible, units should attend training events together, exchange briefings on capabilities and limitations, and coordinate staff actions.

Special Operations

(3) During operations, SOF and CF commanders should understand each other's mission planning cycles, intelligence and operations cycles, and mission approval processes. Mission type orders (task and purpose) are optimal to convey the commander's intent to permit flexibility, initiative, and responsiveness.

b. **Command Relationships**

(1) Properly established and clearly articulated command relationships can directly support decentralization (i.e., decentralized planning and execution for individual missions), foster trust, and aid synergy. These command relationships can broaden the mindset from a very "vertical" focus on receiving and accomplishing activities from the higher commander to a "horizontal"focus, working much more closely with partners.

(2) Successful execution of SO requires clear, responsive C2 by an appropriate SOF C2 element. The limited window of opportunity normally associated with the majority of SOF missions, as well as the sensitive nature of many of these missions, requires a C2 structure that is responsive to the needs of the operational unit. As will be covered in Chapter IV, "Support Considerations for Special Operations Forces," SOF C2 may be uniquely tailored for a specific mission or operation.

c. **Liaisons.** Liaison between SOF and all components of the joint force is essential for effective force employment to coordinate, synchronize, and deconflict SO with CF operations— effective liaison can prevent fratricide, maximize opportunities, and ensure mutual understanding.

For further information on CF-SOF integration and interoperability, refer to USSOCOM Publication 3-33, v.3 , CF/SOF Multi-Service Tactics, Techniques, and Procedures for Conventional Forces and Special Operations Forces Integration and Interoperability, *and JP 3-05.1,* Joint Special Operations Task Force Operations.

6. Coordination and Liaison Elements

SOF commanders have specific elements that facilitate liaison and coordination. They include the special operations command and control element (SOCCE) to command and control, and coordinate SOF activities with CF; the special operations liaison element (SOLE) to provide liaison to the JFACC or appropriate Service component air C2 facility; and SOF liaison officers (LNOs) placed in a variety of locations as necessary to coordinate, synchronize, and deconflict SO within the operational area. All of these elements significantly improve the flow of information, facilitate concurrent planning, and enhance overall mission accomplishment of the joint force.

a. **SOCCE.** The SOCCE is the focal point for the synchronization of SOF activities with conventional force operations. It performs C2 or liaison functions according to mission requirements and as directed by the establishing SOF commander (JFSOCC or CDRJSOTF as appropriate). Its level of authority and responsibility may vary widely. The SOCCE normally is employed when SOF conduct operations in support of a conventional force. It collocates with the command post of the supported force to coordinate, synchronize, and deconflict SO with the operations of the supported force and to ensure communications interoperability with that force. The SOCCE can receive SOF operational, intelligence, and target acquisition reports directly from deployed SOF elements and provide them to the supported component HQ. The JFSOCC, CDRJSOTF, or JSOTF component commanders may attach liaison teams from other SOF elements to the SOCCE as required. The SOCCE remains under the OPCON of the establishing SOF commander. The SOCCE performs the following functions:

(1) As directed, facilitates or exercises C2 of SOF tactical elements attached to, or placed in direct support of, the supported CF commander.

(2) Advises the CF commander on the current situation, missions, capabilities, and limitations of supporting and supported SOF units.

(3) Advises the supporting SOF commander(s) of the supported force commander's current situation, missions, intentions, and requirements.

(4) Provides required secure communications links.

(5) Coordinates and deconflicts SO activities withoperations of the CF.

(6) When linkup between SOF and CF becomes imminent, assists the supported CF commander and staff with SOF linkup planning and execution.

b. **SOLE.** A SOLE is typically a joint team provided by the JFSOCC to the JFACC (if designated) or appropriate Service component air C2 organization, to coordinate, deconflict, and integrate special operations air, surface, and subsurface operations with conventional air operations. The SOLE director works directly for the JFSOCC/CDRJSOTF as a liaison and has no command authority for mission tasking, planning, and execution. The SOLE director places SOF ground, maritime, and air liaison personnel in the joint air operations center (JAOC) to coordinate, deconflict, and synchronize SOF with conventional air operations. The SOLE also provides coordination for the visibility of SOF operations in the air tasking order and the airspace control order. The SOLE must also coordinate appropriate fire support coordination measures between the JAOC and the SOF HQ to help prevent potential for fratricide. A SOLE is tailored as appropriate (see Figure III-4).

c. **SOF LNOs.** SOF LNOs report to the SOF commander or SOF component commander and are dispatched to applicable conventional JTF components to ensure the timely exchange of necessary operational and support information to aid mission execution and preclude fratricide, duplication of effort, disruption of ongoing operations, or loss of intelligence sources. SOF LNOs may assist in the coordination of fire support, overflight, aerial refueling, targeting, deception, MISO, CAO, and other operational issues based on current and future SO missions. These efforts are crucial to the JFC's unity of effort, tempo, and coordination of limited resources and assets.

7. Joint Special Operations Area

a. Coordination and deconfliction with CF are always critical concerns for SOF commanders. SOF are often employed prior to the arrival of CF. Effective coordination is vital in the transition from advance force operations involving SOF to follow-on operations and in ensuring that the timing and tempo of the overall campaign is maintained.

b. The **JFC may establish a JSOA,** which is a restricted area of land, sea, and airspace assigned by a JFC to the commander of a joint special operations force to conduct SO activities. The commander of SOF may further assign a specific area or sector within the JSOA to a subordinate commander for mission execution. The scope and duration of the SOF mission, friendly and hostile situation, and politico-military considerations all influence the number, composition, and sequencing of SOF deployed into a JSOA. It may be limited in size to accommodate a discrete DA mission or may be extensive enough to allow a continuing broad range of UW operations. JFCs may use a JSOA to delineate and facilitate simultaneous use of CF and SOF in the same general operational area. When a JSOA is designated, the JFSOCC (or CDRJSOTF) is the supported commander within the designated JSOA.

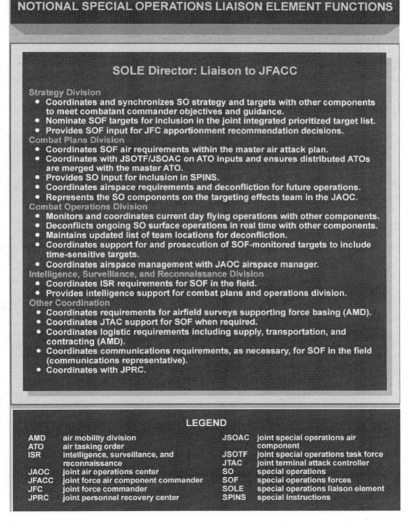

Figure III-4. Notional Special Operations Liaison Element Functions.

c. Establishment of a designated JSOA for SOF to conduct unilateral operations assists in the ease of control of SO and the prevention of fratricide.

8. Interorganizational Coordination

a. Interagency coordination is as integral to SO as it is conventional operations, and fostering personal relationships between SOF commanders and interorganizational leaders and professional relations between both staffs should be a routine objective during military engagement activities.

b. A proven model in attaining unity of effort with interorganizational partners is the complementary character of the DOS embassy mission strategic plans and country operational plans, and a GCC's theater campaign plan.

c. Interpersonal communication skills that emphasize consultation, persuasion, compromise, and consensus are the means to obtain unified action in a military-civilian effort. Successful commanders and staff build personal relationships to inspire trust and confidence. The challenges of gaining harmony and creating synergy among the engaged USG agencies and multinational partners are greater as there are no clear authorities directing the relationship. If tasked by the GCC/CJTF, a CDRJSOTF may be the coordinating authority for some form of interorganizational coordination at what could be characterized as the operational level, and responsible for the unified action down through the tactical level.

For further information on interagency considerations, refer to JP 3-08, Interorganizational Coordination During Joint Operations.

9. Multinational Coordination

SOF operate with multinational forces (MNFs), i.e., forces belonging to a coalition or alliance, on a routine and recurring basis. US SOF assess, train, advise, assist, and operate with a plethora of multinational foreign special operations units. They also do the same with many multinational conventional force units, in both supported and supporting relationships.

a. SOF training or operating with MNFs is typically the result of tasking by a CCDR in coordination with the appropriate DOS representatives and other interagency partners. Coordination of national level direction among the MNF partners should be anticipated at the national and theater levels.

b. **Command Considerations.** Any control of SOF operating elements transferred to a foreign commander must include an appropriate SOF command element in the chain of command for direct C2 of the SOF operating elements.

c. For MNF operations, rules of engagement (ROE) may be different for the non-US military units, than for US units. That could result in some form of operating limitations. US military forces may have to follow more restrictive ROE (US or multinational) dependent upon agreed command relationships; however, they always retain their right to self-defense per US ROE. ROE typically is coordinated with all MNF participants. US ROE must be coordinated by the supported JFC.

Special Operations

d. SOF may be tasked to liaise with and advise units of a MNF, providing the primary means of communications and C2 with the MNF operational HQ. This could mean the SOF would require significant additional communications equipment to facilitate the C2 and coordination responsibilities.

e. MNF operations typically require some degree of US logistics support to be coordinated.

f. Although capable in many foreign languages, for MNF operations the SOF may require interpreters to facilitate communication and coordination.

g. Foreign disclosure will always be a consideration for coordination and release of intelligence and other information.

h. There should be a multinational coordination center, especially if the MNF is operating under a parallel command structure, to facilitate most, if not all coordination efforts among the MNF.

For further information on multinational coordination and operations, refer to JP 3-16, Multinational Operations.

IV. SUPPORT CONSIDERATIONS FOR SPECIAL OPERATIONS FORCES

"The operational effectiveness of our deployed forces cannot be, and never has been, achieved without being enabled by our joint Service partners. The support Air Force, Army, Marine, and Navy engineers, [explosive ordnance disposal] technicians, intelligence analysts, and the numerous other professions that contribute to SOF [special operations forces], have substantially increased our capabilities and effectiveness throughout the world."

Admiral Eric T. Olson
December 2008

1. Introduction

SOF support must be tailored to specific mission requirements, yet flexible enough to respond to changing employment parameters. The joint character of SO requires support arrangements across Service lines with emphasis on unique support required in order to sustain independent and remote operations. Further, SOF must be able to exploit information derived from the full range of available multinational, national, theater, and tactical intelligence, surveillance, and reconnaissance support systems.

2. Intelligence Support

All-source, fused intelligence is vital in identifying relevant targets, COA development, and mission planning/execution. SO require detailed planning, often by relatively small units. Consequently, intelligence requirements are normally greater in scope and depth than that of CF. Joint intelligence preparation of the operational environment (JIPOE) provides the foundation for SO intelligence production. Like CF operations, SO intelligence analysis focuses on the operational area and the area of interest (AOI); however, the strategic nature of SO frequently incorporates an expanded AOI. SO planning typically requires a comprehensive analysis of the geopolitical and socioeconomic situation in the operational area and AOI to ensure all factors that may affect mission accomplishment are considered. SO, having a reduced margin of error due to the small size of teams, require greater depth in target intelligence and greater detail in JIPOE to ensure success and avoid casualties.

a. **Interface with National and Theater Intelligence Assets.** The ability to interface with theater/national intelligence systems and assets is critical for SO mission success. The combatant command joint intelligence operations center (JIOC) is the focal point for intelligence activities in support of joint operations with additional support from the Defense Intelligence Operations Coordination Center (DIOCC). Joint force requests for information (RFIs) are forwarded to the combatant command JIOC. If the JIOC is unable to respond, RFIs are forwarded to the DIOCC. The DIOCC will then interface with other DOD intelligence agencies or the national intelligence community through the National Intelligence Coordination Center (NICC) to provide support. If the DIOCC determines that the information required has not been produced by any agency in the intelligence community, the DIOCC will coordinate with the combatant command JIOC and NICC to recommend an appropriate strategy to collect, process, analyze, produce, and disseminate the required information. A JSOTF, when formed, will have access to these same theater and national interfaces through the combatant command JIOC and the DIOCC. Additionally, a JSOTF may be augmented with a national intelligence support team comprised of representatives from many national intelligence and combat support agencies.

b. **All-Source Intelligence.** The nature of many SO objectives and tactics requires all-source intelligence support that is often more detailed than that required in conventional operations. SOF often use intelligence information to avoid adversary forces, regardless of size or composition, as opposed to intelligence information that would allow CF to engage the adversary (see Figure IV-1).

c. **Expanded Focus.** Intelligence support for SOF conducting military engagement, security cooperation, crisis response, or limited contingencies requires various intelligence disciplines to widen their focus. This includes political, informational, economic, and cultural institutions and relationships as well as adversary, friendly force, and target specific data including the use of civil information management and other open-source information avenues. This is particularly true during FID and when tasked to participate in noncombatant evacuation operations.

d. **Sensitivity to HN and Adversary Collection Efforts.** SO missions are particularly sensitive to HN and adversary collection efforts. Counterintelligence support and OPSEC assist in protecting sensitive SO missions.

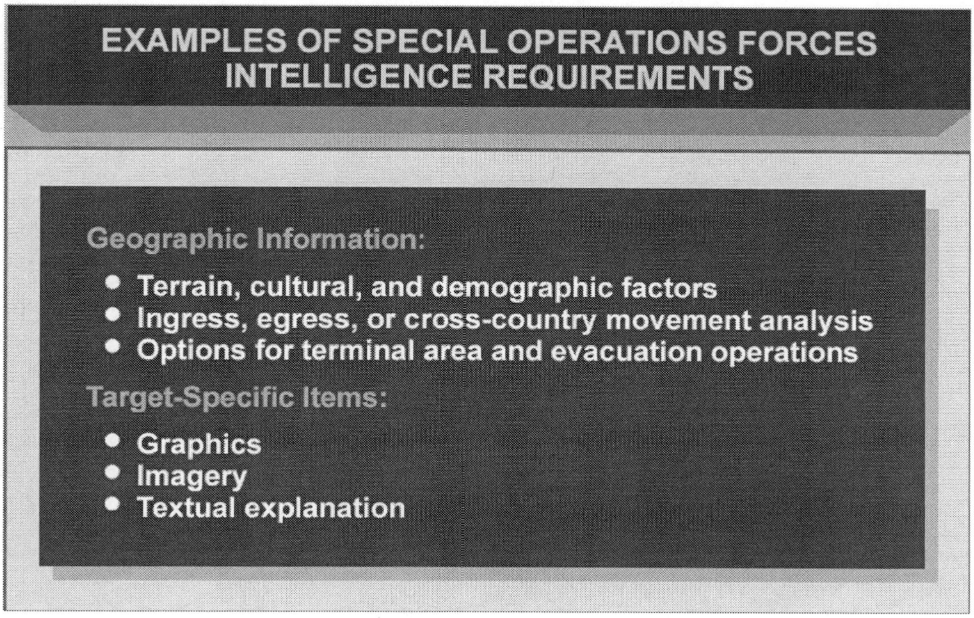

EXAMPLES OF SPECIAL OPERATIONS FORCES INTELLIGENCE REQUIREMENTS

Geographic Information:

- Terrain, cultural, and demographic factors
- Ingress, egress, or cross-country movement analysis
- Options for terminal area and evacuation operations

Target-Specific Items:

- Graphics
- Imagery
- Textual explanation

Figure IV-1. Examples of Special Operations Forces Intelligence Requirements.

e. **Geospatial Intelligence (GEOINT) Support.** GEOINT support can provide timely, complete, and accurate information to help SOF with the visualization of the operational environment. SOF commanders use GEOINT to help determine friendly and adversary COAs and to plan for deployment of SOF and key weapons systems. GEOINT contingency planning identifies the AOI and determines GEOINT requirements for SO activities and weapons systems. It also determines current availability for resources to meet those requirements, determines risk, and then develops a production strategy to address shortfalls. During crisis action planning (CAP), the requirement to plan GEOINT support for crisis response operations depends greatly upon the scope of the mission, how much GEOINT can be adapted from existing contingency plans, and the total time available for GEOINT to be included in the CAP process. When plans call for working in a multinational force or with HN forces, early consideration should be given to developing and using releasable intelligence products, to the maximum extent consistent with security considerations. This will facilitate a common operational picture.

f. **SOF Support to National and Theater Human Information Requirements.** While SO can be informed by national and theater intelligence assets, SO fill a critical gap in providing information that is not available through technical means. SOF's presence in denied or politically sensitive areas can provide enhanced situational awareness to a JFC that would not otherwise be available.

For further information on intelligence support, refer to JP 2-01, Joint and National Intelligence Support to Military Operations, *JP 2-01.3,* Joint Intelligence Preparation of the Operational Environment, *and JP 3-05.1,* Joint Special Operations Task Force Operations.

For further information on GEOINT, refer to JP 2-03, Geospatial Intelligence Support to Joint Operations.

3. Operational Contract Support

Operational contract support is as integral to SO as it is to conventional operations. The continual introduction of high-tech equipment, coupled with force structure and manning limitations, and high operating tempo mean that SOF may be augmented with contracted support, including contingency contractor employees and all tiers of subcontractor employees who are specifically authorized through their contract to accompany the force and have protected status in accordance with international conventions (i.e., contractors authorized to accompany the force). To do this, contract support integration and contractor management must be integrated into military planning and operations. Early integration of these planning considerations also allows for any unique security clearance or OPSEC concerns related to the SO.

For more information regarding operational contract support, see JP 4-10, Operational Contract Support.

4. Host-Nation Support

Host-nation support (HNS) is that civil and/or military assistance rendered by a nation to foreign forces within its territory based on agreements mutually concluded between nations. For SO, HNS must be weighed against OPSEC considerations, mission requirements and duration, and the operational environment. HNS is a key common-user logistics area of concern.

a. HNS may often play an important role in reducing the military logistic footprint in theater, thus allowing the deployment of increased combat capabilities early in the operation. HNS can also provide long-term logistic support, thus freeing up key military logistic capabilities for other contingencies.

b. Some considerations for HNS:

   (1) Authority for negotiations must be obtained through the supported JFC (to include the supported GCC) and through the appropriate US COM channels.

   (2) Whenever possible, HNS agreements should include the authority for the CDRJSOTF to coordinate directly with the HN for support, acquisition, and use of facilities and real estate.

   (3) Every effort should be made to obtain language support for negotiations with local nationals.

   (4) A legal advisor experienced in HNS should be involved in the HNS agreements process.

   (5) It is critical to determine a lead agency to contract and negotiate HNS.

   (6) To optimize effective HNS, there should be centralized planning and coordination of HNS functions (i.e., identification of requirements and procurement).

   (7) Especially for SOF, the movement/distribution and security of applicable HNS items must be considered, based on the operational environment.

For additional information regarding HNS, see JP 3-05.1, Joint Special Operations Task Force Operations, *and JP 4-0,* Joint Logistics. *Refer to DODD 2010.9,*

Acquisition and Cross-Servicing Agreements, *for policy for the acquisition from and transfer to authorized foreign governments of logistics support, supplies, and services.*

5. Logistic Support

GCCs and their Service component commanders, in coordination with the CDRTSOC, are responsible for ensuring that effective and responsive support systems are developed and provided for assigned/attached SOF. The CDRTSOC, or the JFSOCC/CDRJSOTF, when a JTF is established, validates logistic requirements for SOF in theater for the GCC. To the extent possible, SOF logistic requirements should be identified during the contingency planning process. Logistic support for SOF units can be provided through one or more of the following:

a. **Service Support.** The logistic support of SOF units is the responsibility of their parent Service, except where otherwise provided for by support agreements or other directives. This responsibility exists regardless of whether the SOF unit requiring support is assigned to the Service component, the TSOC, JFSOCC, or a JSOTF. SOF Service-common logistic support includes equipment, material, supplies, and services adopted by a military Service for use by its own forces and their activities. These include standard military items, base operating support, and the supplies and services provided by a Service to support and sustain its own forces, including those forces assigned to the combatant commands. Items and services defined as Service-common by one Service are not necessarily Service-common for all other Services.

b. **Joint In-Theater Support.** The majority of SOF missions require joint logistic planning and execution. When a theater Service component cannot satisfy its Service SOF support requirements, the GCC will determine if another Service component can do so through common or joint servicing arrangements. Joint logistic arrangements may also be used when more effective than normal Service support.

c. **Nonstandard Support.** When operations involving SOF impose time, geographic, and/or resource constraints on the theater support infrastructure, making it impractical for the theater to provide the requisite support to SOF, the GCC may request from CDRUSSOCOM the deployment of organic USSOCOM combat service support assets.

d. **SO-Peculiar Support.** SO-peculiar logistic support includes equipment, materials, supplies, and services required for SO missions for which there is no Service-common requirement. These are limited to items and services initially designed for, or used by, SOF until adopted for Service-common use by one or more Service. Modifications are approved by CDRUSSOCOM for application to standard items and services used by the Services, and items and services identified as critically urgent for the immediate accomplishment of a special operations mission. This support will be provided via USSOCOM Service componentlogistic infrastructures and in coordination with theater Service components.

e. **HNS.** Countries with or without a government infrastructure may only be able to provide limited logistics support.

Joint Publication 3-05

For further information on SOF logistic support, refer to JP 4-0, Joint Logistics, *and JP 3-05.1,* Joint Special Operations Task Force Operations .

6. Health Service Support

SOF teams frequently operate in remote areas and therefore, are exposed to health threats not normally seen in the other areas of the respective HNs. As a consequence, proactive force health protection is critical for mission success and preservation of high-value SOF assets. SOF will often operate in theaters that are underdeveloped with little or no health care support structure. Point-to-point movement to designated Medical Treatment Facilities is standard while medical regulating and strategic aeromedical evacuation (AE) might be required and should be part of the contingency planning process.

a. **Austere SOF Support Structure.** SOF health service support is characterized by an austere structure and a limited number of medical personnel with enhanced medical skills. SOF medical personnel often provide emergency treatment and a basic level of medical care at the operational team levelwith organic medical assets . Additional medical support and patient movement (see Figure IV-2) provided to SOF units in the operational area can be planned and conducted by SOF medical personnel. Not all SOF missions require SOF-trained medical assets. SOF medical assets are limited and may require support from conventional units. Casualty evacuation (CASEVAC) for SOF personnel is the transport of casualties by any expedient means possible. SOF medical personnel perform CASEVAC missions, forward of the intermediate staging base (ISB), on opportune aircraft or other means of transport, back to the ISB or a predetermined point where AE assets are located. Requests for medical regulating should be submitted to the appropriate patient movement requirements center after competent medical authority attests to the need to move the patient. AE is conducted once the casualty is regulated into the patient movement system. AE is performed using fixed-wing aircraft and AE trained medical crews. It is the movement of patients under medical supervision to and between medical treatment facilities. SOF units have varying degrees of first responder (Role 1) capabilities and limited forward resuscitative (Role 2) capabilities. SOF do not have organic theater hospitalization (Role 3) or definitive care (Role 4) capabilities readily available to them and must rely on either available theater health service support assets or local HN capabilities when access to theater hospitalization (Role3)care is an urgent necessity.

b. **Conventional Support Structure.** Provision of medical support beyond SOF capabilities depends on the thoroughness of advanced planning so that the conventional medical support structure umbrella is extended to cover the limited organic capability or to meet requirements for additional medical assets (such as surgical intervention, evacuation, and expanded medical logistics). SOF medical units deploy with initial assets to support operational planning requirements. Deployed medical resupply is the responsibility of the theater medical logistics system. SOF and theater medical planners need to establish a responsive medical logistics resupply process utilizing the theater medical logistics system. Certain

Special Operations 101

operations may also require special security requirements to be put in place to not compromise the identification of SOF personnel upon entry into the conventional medical system.

For further information on health service support, refer to JP 4-02, Health Service Support, *and JP 3-05.1,* Joint Special Operations Task Force Operations .

7. Communications Systems Support

a. **Global Support.** Communications systems support to SOF normally are global, secure, and jointly interoperable. It must be flexible so that it can be tailored to specific SO missions and it must add value to the SOF operational capability. Communications systems support the full range of SO worldwide. SOF must be able to communicate anywhere and anytime using the full range of national capabilities required to support the mission. Therefore, SOF operational units have a variety of methods for communicating, reporting, and querying available resources, regardless of geographic location.

b. **Multiple and Varied Systems.** SOF communications support consists of multiple and varied groups of systems, procedures, personnel, and equipment that operate in diverse manners and at different echelons, from the national to the tactical levels. Communications systems have to support discrete as well as collective functions. SOF missions are normally controlled at the lowest operational level that can accomplish the needed coordination, although political considerations may require control at the national level. SOF communicationssystems are set up tooffer seamless connectivity.

c. **Interoperable Systems.** SOF communications systems employed for a given operation should be selected based on their ability to be interoperable at the appropriate security level with the systems deployed by US CF, joint commands, multinational units, and US commercial networks to facilitate the seamless transport of critical information and common services. They should also have the flexibility to integrate not only with state-of-the-art systems, but also be capable of integrating with less sophisticated equipment often found in less developed nations. Interoperability includes attaining commonality, compatibility, and standardization of communications systems.

d. **CDRUSSOCOM Responsibilities.** CDRUSSOCOM, as do each of the Services, has the following communications responsibilities:

(1) To provide, operate, and maintain communication facilities organic to SOF, including organic Service elements.

(2) To provide, operate, and maintain interoperable and compatible communicationssystems.

(3) To provide the capability for interface of non-Defense Information Systems Network facilities.

(4) To provide the combatant commands with SO communications systems and connectivity for SOF assigned to that command for inclusion in contingency planning.

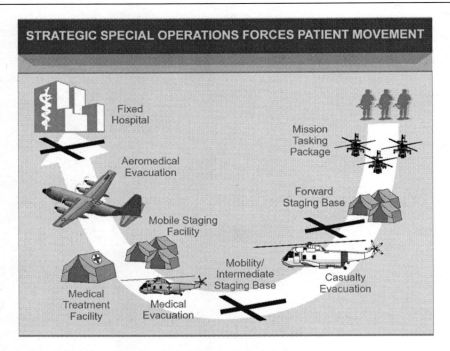

Figure IV-2. Strategic Special Operations Forces Patient Movement.

For further information on communications support of SOF, refer to JP 3-05.1, Joint Special Operations Task Force Operations, *and JP 6-0,* Joint Communications System.

8. Public Affairs Support

a. **Diplomatic and Political Sensitivity of SO.** The diplomatic and political sensitivity of many SO mandates that thorough and accurate PA guidance be developed during the operational planning stage and approved for use in advance of most SO.

b. **Accurate Reflection of the SO Mission.** PA planning must accurately reflect the objective of the mission to domestic audiences consistent with the overall MISO and CMO effort, and with strategic, operational, and tactical OPSEC requirements. The commander should develop proposed PA guidance that is coordinated with supporting commands and government agencies, as appropriate, prior to forwarding that guidance to the Assistant Secretary of Defense (Public Affairs) for approval.

For further information on PA support, refer to JP 3-61, Public Affairs, *and JP 3-05.1,* Joint Special Operations Task Force Operations.

9. Combat Camera Support

a. **Combat camera** provides still and video documentary products that support MISO and other SO missions. Many combat camera teams supporting SOF are specially equipped with night vision and digital image transmission capabilities. Combat camera also provides gun camera image processing for theater and national use. Combat camera imagery is used to portray the true nature of US operations to multinational partners and civilian populaces, as well as adversaries, and to counter adversary disinformation with on-screen or gun camera evidence. The SOF link to combat camera support normally is through the supported GCC's IO cell and the visual information planner.

b. **Visual Information.** The coordination of visual information is an important function that leverages this extensive cross-element support. Each of the following contributes some type of imagery—all of which are combined to shape a comprehensive visualization package for special operations missions. Visual information is derived from a variety of sources such as unmanned aircraft collected imagery, photo journalist collected imagery, PA imagery, intelligence related imagery, satellite imagery, individual soldier collected imagery, gun camera imagery, as well as combat camera products. The visual information function supports the overall planning and implementation of SO and is especially valuable to a commander's communications strategy. The communication strategy is the JFC's strategy for coordinating and synchronizing themes, messages, images, and actions to support objectives and to ensure the integrity and consistency of themes and messages to the lowest tactical level.

10. Legal Support

SO missions frequently involve a unique set of complex issues. There are federal laws and executive orders, federal agency publications and directives, the law of armed conflict, and ROE that may affect SO missions as well as the SO joint planning and targeting processes. These guidelines become especially critical during sensitive contingency missions when international and domestic laws, treaty provisions, and political agreements may affect mission planning and execution. SOF commanders must seek legal review during all levels of planning and execution of SO missions, to include planning of the ROE.

For further information on legal support, refer to JP 1-04, Legal Support, *and JP 3-05.1,* Joint Special Operations Task Force Operations.

11. Protection

a. The protection of the force is an essential consideration. Protection focuses on conserving the SOF fighting potential, whether operating independently, or as part of a larger joint force in a major operation/campaign. The four primary ways: active defensive measures that protect the joint force, its information, its bases, necessary infrastructure, and lines of communications from an adversary'spassive defensive measures that make friendly forces, systems, and facilities difficult to locate, strike, and destroy; applying technology and procedures to reduce the risk of fratricide; and emergency management and response to reduce the loss of personnel and capabilities due to accidents, health threats, and natural disasters. As the JFC's mission requires, the protection function also extends beyond force protection to encompass protection of US civilians; the forces, systems, and civil infrastructure of friendly nations; and OGAs, IGOs, and NGOs. For force protection, typically each GCC has TACON of US forces in their AOR.

b. Protection considerations include basic force security; active and passive air and missile defense; OPSEC; computer network defense (CND); information assurance (IA); electronic protection; personnel recovery; CBRN operations; antiterrorism support; combat identification; survivability; safety; and force health protection.

c. SOF planners should ensure their planning and supported theater plans include as adequate provisions for protection as they would for intelligence, sustainment, communications, etc.

For more detailed information regarding protection, see JP 3-0, Joint Operations.

12. Fire Support

SOF may require long-range, surface-based, joint fire support in remote locations or for targets well beyond the land, maritime, and amphibious operational force area of operations. SOF liaison elements coordinate fire support through both external and SOF channels. SOF liaison elements (e.g., SOCCE and SOLE) provide SOF expertise to coordinate, synchronize, and deconflict SOF fire support. Interoperable communications and detailed procedures between fire support providers and SOF operating deep within enemy territory must be considered. Comprehensive fire support planning between SOF and supporting elements will facilitate rapid, responsive, and accurate mission execution.

For further information on fire support, refer to JP 3-09, Joint Fire Support.

13. Air Support

In addition to their organic air capabilities for infiltration, exfiltration, resupply, and precision fire support, SOF often requires conventional air support that requires timely and detailed planning and coordination. Air support is typically provided by the JFACC (or an Air Force component commander), and the JFSOCC/CDRJSOTF normally provides a SOLE to the JFACC at the JAOC. In addition to helping to deconflict and coordinate SO with the JFACC, the SOLE helps coordinate SO requests for air support. Air support can include intelligence, surveillance, and reconnaissance, airlift, close air support, air refueling, EW, etc., and the use of SOF or CF joint terminal attack controllers (JTACs), TACPs, and/or the elements and capabilities of an Air Force air support operations center (ASOC) located with an Army component command. JTACs/TACPs can work directly for SOF units supporting various missions. ASOCs can help the SOF commander integrate and synchronize use of air power to support SO. Elements provided to SOF units may require additional training or equipment to effectively and safely facilitate air support during SO.

14. Maritime Support

Maritime support is provided by the joint force maritime component commander, the Navy component commander, and/or the Marine Corps component commander. Maritime support includes fire support, seabasing operations, deception, and deterrence. Maritime support, such as SOF helicopters landing on Navy ships, typically requires advanced planning and coordination because of technical and safety issues. Additionally, the commander, amphibious task force and the commander, landing force, may also provide amphibious support for the MARSOF and other SOF units. The unique nature of SOF equipment and operational requirements (e.g., communications, weapons, and the need for compartmentalized planning spaces) further reinforce the requirement for early coordination.

For more information on helicopter employment from Navy ships, see JP 3-04, Joint Shipboard Helicopter Operations.

15. Space Support

With the exception of intelligence provided by national technical means, space support for SOF is provided through the USSTRATCOM Joint Functional Component Command for Space upon request by the supported CCDR.

a. For theater level support, Services assign space operators to various joint and Service echelons. JFCs may assign space experts to the joint component commanders' staffs. JFCs and their components request space services and capabilities early in the planning process to ensure effective and efficient use of space assets. Each GCC has a network of space technicians and subject matter expert staff officers, resident on staffs at multiple echelons, who serve as theater advisors for space capabilities (national, military, civil, commercial, and foreign). These individuals concentrate primarily on working the detailed activities of theater space operations based on coordination with the JFC's oordinating authority in developing, collecting, and prioritizing space requirements. Several DOD and national agencies deploy theater support teams that can provide additional space services and capabilities.

b. Space support personnel can assist SOF commanders and staff in understanding the capabilities, limitations, and effective application of space systems, and ensure that SOF support requirements are clearly understood. Space based support to SOF can include: precision navigation and/or geopositioning, global communications, global intelligence collection, surveillance and warning, meteorological support, imagery for geospatial support and targeting, blue force tracking data, and denying adversary use of space-based capabilities (see Figure IV-3). Satellite threat advisories can provide additional mission security by influencing SOF operational timing.

For further information on space support, refer to JP 3-14, Space Operations, *and JP 3-05.1,* Joint Special Operations Task Force Operations.

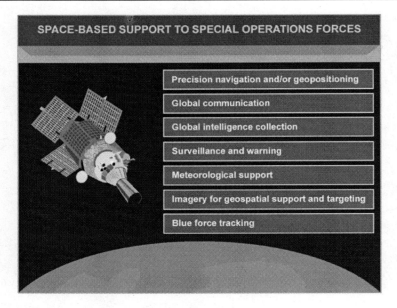

Figure IV-3. Space-Based Support to Special Operations Forces.

16. Meteorological and Oceanographic Support

a. **Use of Environmental Data.** Environmental information should be integrated in the SOF commander's -making process from initial planning to execution (e.g., jointdecision operational planning process and intelligence preparation of the battlespace). Meteorological and oceanographic (METOC) data can provide information such as studies of general climatology, operational climatology, hydrography, and specific weather forecasts such as mission execution forecast for the operational area focused on operationally significant METOC thresholds. This information can be used by the commander to choose the best windows of opportunity to execute, support, and sustain specific SOF operations.

b. **Exploitation of METOC Conditions.** Potentially, an execution decision may be based on exploiting certain weather and METOC conditions to provide the best advantages in conducting operations while avoiding environmental conditions that will adversely impact operations. SOF units train to exploit every advantage, and operating at the limits of their capabilities, frequently require extraordinarily precise, fine-scale METOC products.

c. **Environmental Effects on Space Operations.** With increased military reliance on space capabilities, the SOF commander must also be kept informed of environmental effects on space operations. METOC support personnel can provide information that will allow the SOF commander to plan for the possibility of the loss of one or more critical space-based systems, such asprecision navigation, timing, and communications systems.

For further information on METOC support, refer to JP 3-59, Meteorological and Oceanographic Operations, *and JP 3-05.1,* Joint Special Operations Task Force Operations.

17. Cyberspace Support

Cyberspace crosses all the physical domains and provides military advantage to both SOF and adversaries alike. Cyberspace operations in support of SO can often be conducted remotely, thus reducing the SOF footprint and contributing to freedom of action within a given operational area. The Services maintain cyberspace forces, some of whom are dedicated to providing specific support to SOF. In some cases, those forces are apportioned to SOF directly, while in others, they are simply aligned in a supporting role to SOF.

18. Information Operations Support

IO are integral to successful military operations and especially when conducting SO. The full impact of IO on friendly, neutral, and hostile forces should be considered in the communication strategy of the supported JFC with the goal of achieving and maintaining information superiority for joint and friendly forces. IO are described as the integrated employment of the core capabilities of EW, CNO, MISO, MILDEC, and OPSEC, in concert with specified supporting and related capabilities to influence, disrupt, corrupt, or usurp adversary human and automated decision making while protecting our own.

a. **IO is a SOF core activity, and also integral to the successful execution of many SO.** MISO is a SOF core activity and a core IO capability, as is the IO related capability of CMO, often involved with CA operations, another SOF core activity. SO may require support from any combination of core, supporting, or related IO capabilities, so the JFC's IO cell should include a SOF representative. SOF require IO support, whether SOF are employed independently or in conjunction with CF.

(1) OPSEC and MILDEC are key parts of setting the conditions for operational success of SO. These efforts are central to achieving surprise, helping to isolate the target area, and will also be important enablers for gaining control of the operational environment and neutralizing enemy forces.

(a) OPSEC attempts to deny critical information about friendly forces to the adversary. SOF preparing for deployment can have distinct signatures. Masking the movement of forces to staging bases and to the operational area is essential. These movements may not be totally hidden; however, such detail as the composition of the forces or the time and location of the deployment or infiltration should be concealed. The object is to surprise, confuse, or paralyze the enemy. OPSEC procedures must be planned, practiced, and enforced during training, movement, and operations.

For further details on OPSEC, refer to JP 3-13.3, Operations Security.

(b) MILDEC misleads the adversary as to friendly military capabilities, intentions, and operations, thereby causing the adversary to take specific actions (or inactions) that may contribute to the accomplishment of the friendly mission. MILDEC operations must be closely coordinated with the overall operational scheme of maneuver and other IO efforts. The deception operation will have little effect if it is compromised by poor OPSEC or conflicts with concurrent MISO. Successful military deceptions require sufficient resources, leadership, and linked objectives and goals from the strategic to tactical level.

For further details on MILDEC, refer to JP 3-13.4, Military Deception.

(2) EW includes any military action involving the use of electromagnetic and directed energy to control the electromagnetic spectrum or to attack the enemy. The JFC's plan must be developed to ensure complementary use of assets and weapons systems to effectively disrupt and/or destroy enemy C2 and weapons systems, while protecting joint force capabilities.

See JP 3-13.1, Electronic Warfare, *for additional detail on EW.*

(3) CNO stems from the use of networked computers and supporting information technology infrastructure systems by military and civilian organizations. CNO are cyberspace operations that may very easily be used in support of SO. CNO, along with EW, is used to attack, deceive, degrade, disrupt, deny, exploit, and defend electronic information and infrastructure. For the purpose of military operations, CNO are divided into computer network attack (CNA), CND, and related computer network exploitation (CNE) enabling operations. CNA consists of actions taken through the use of computer networks to disrupt, deny, degrade, or destroy information resident in computers and computer networks, or the computers and networks themselves. CND involves actions taken through the use of computer networks to protect, monitor, analyze, detect, and respond to unauthorized activity within DOD information systems and computer networks. CND actions not only protect DOD systems from an external adversary but also from exploitation from within, and are now a necessary function in all military operations. CNE is enabling operations and intelligence collection capabilities conducted through the use of computer networks to gather data from target or adversary automated information systems or networks. However, it must be understood that many irregular adversaries use the Internet as a means of C2 and for planning purposes, so for example, one form of CNO (e.g., CNE) may be possible when another (e.g., CNA) would not.

b. A goal of a JFC is to shape the information environment to achieve information superiority. The JFC should strive to create and/or sustain desired and measurable effects on foreign TAs; while protecting and defending the JFC's own forces, actions, information, and information systems. As part of IO, the JFC ensures SOF IO requirements are worked into the overall IO planning and execution. SO planning should include considerations for IO support based on the communication strategy of the supported JFC.

c. IO capabilities will also play an integral role in isolating a SO target, whether that isolation is from nearby enemy military forces, or from enemy C2 nodes and centers, both inside and outside the operational area. For example, synchronized CNO and EW, supported by physical attack on a C2 network, could play a decisive role in this isolation.

d. Supporting IO capabilities (IA, physical security, physical attack, counterintelligence, and combat camera) have military purposes other than IO, but they either operate in the information environment or have impact on the information environment.

Special Operations

e. **Related Information Operations Capabilities**

(1) **Defense support to public diplomacy (DSPD)** consists of activities and measures taken by DOD components, not solely in the area of IO, to support and facilitate public diplomacy efforts of the USG. DSPD requires coordination among interagency partners and should be part of the JFC's

(2) **PA** activities are separate, but not isolated from IO. Planning for SO, both by the JFC and SOF, should include PA considerations based on the desired and actual effects of the SO. PA planning should anticipate the potential detection by the enemy and the media of all military operations, with the possible exception of small covert operations. Likewise, PA planning should anticipate potential responses to an unsuccessful operation or adverse effects such as collateral damage.

(3) Properly executed **CMO** in an operational area can reduce potential friction points between the civilian population and the joint force, specifically by minimizing civilian interference with military operations and limiting the impact of military operations on the populace. CMO encompass the activities taken by a commander to establish and maintain effective relations between military forces and civil authorities, the general population, and other civil institutions in friendly, neutral, or hostile areas where those forces are employed. CA forces and units are specifically organized, trained, and equipped to conduct CA operations in support of CMO.

For further details on CMO, refer to JP 3-57, Civil-Military Operations.

19. Multinational Support

Multinational support to SOF complements HNS and depends on mission and capability requirements.

a. Support may range from broad assistance to highly structured and integrated support from multinational CF and multinational SOF. Common examples include information and intelligence sharing; providing liaison teams and support to planning efforts; materiel assistance; basing, access, and overflight permission; humanitarian assistance; and linguists and cultural advice and awareness. Multinational CF and multinational SOF have proven invaluable in aiding and augmenting troop rotation, supporting strategic movement, providing medical evacuation, conducting FID, and participating in multinational support teams.

b. Planners must anticipate requirements and prepare for multinational support SOF, sometimes years in advance and on a recurring basis. Various means of preparation include establishment of HQ multinational coordination cells; establishment and use of senior national representatives and defense attachés; specialized predeployment/ interoperability training; various agreements (e.g., communications security and cross servicing agreements); and combined training and exercises. In some cases, a joint exchange combined training program might be used to share skills and improve operational capabilities between US and HN forces.

APPENDIX A

References

The development of JP 3-05 is based upon the following primary references.

1. General

    a.   Title 10, USC, as amended.

    b.   *Unified Command Plan.*

2. Department of Defense

    a.   DOD Directive 5100.1, *Functions of the Department of Defense and its Major Components.*

    b.   Department of Defense Instruction 6000.11, *Patient Movement.*

3. Chairman of the Joint Chiefs of Staff

    a.   Chairman of the Joint Chiefs of Staff Instruction (CJCSI) 3110.01G, *Joint Strategic Capabilities Plan (JSCP).*

    b.   CJCSI 3110.05D, *Joint Psychological Operations Supplement to the JSCP.*

    c.   CJCSI 3110.06, *Special Operations Supplemental to JSCP.*

    d.   CJCSI 3110.12D, *Civil Affairs Supplement to the JSCP.*

    e.   CJCSI 3210.01A, *Joint Information Warfare Policy.*

    f.   CJCSI 3214.01, *Military Support to Foreign Consequence Management Operations.*

    g.   Joint Chiefs of Staff Memorandum 71-87, *Mission and Functions of the US Special Operations Command.*

    h.   JP 1, *Doctrine for the Armed Forces of the United States.*

    i.   JP 1-02, *Department of Defense Dictionary of Military and Associated Terms.*

    j.   JP 1-04, *Legal Support to Military Operations.*

    k.   JP 2-0, *Joint Intelligence.*

    l.   JP 2-01, *Joint and National Intelligence Support to Military Operations.*

    m.   JP 2-01.3, *Joint Intelligence Preparation of the Operational Environment.*

    n.   JP 2-03, *Geospatial Intelligence Support to Joint Operations.*

    o.   JP 3-0, *Joint Operations.*

    p.   JP 3-05.1, *Joint Special Operations Task Force Operations.*

    q.   JP 3-07.2, *Antiterrorism.*

    r.   JP 3-07.3, *Peace Operations.*

    s.   JP 3-07.4, *Joint Counterdrug Operations.*

    t.   JP 3-08, *Interorganizational Coordination During Joint Operations.*

    u.   JP 3-09, *Joint Fire Support.*

    v.   JP 3-13, *Information Operations.*

    w.   JP 3-13.1, *Electronic Warfare.*

    x.   JP 3-13.2, *Military Information Support Operations.*

Special Operations

y. JP 3-13.3, *Operations Security.*
z. JP 3-13.4, *Military Deception.*
aa. JP 3-14, *Space Operations.*
bb. JP 3-22, *Foreign Internal Defense.*
cc. JP 3-24, *Counterinsurgency Operations.*
dd. JP 3-26, *Counterterrorism.*
ee. JP 3-29, *Foreign Humanitarian Assistance.*
ff. JP 3-33, *Joint Task Force Headquarters.*
gg. JP 3-40, *Combating Weapons of Mass Destruction.*
hh. JP 3-50, *Personnel Recovery.*
ii. JP 3-57, *Civil-Military Operations.*
jj. JP 3-59, *Meteorological and Oceanographic Operations.*
kk. JP 3-61, *Public Affairs.*
ll. JP 4-0, *Joint Logistics.*
mm. JP 4-02, *Health Service Support.*
nn. JP 4-10, *Operational Contract Support.*
oo. JP 5-0, *Joint Operation Planning.*
pp. JP 6-0, *Communications System Support.*

4. United States Special Operations Command and Service Publications

a. US Army Field Manual 3-05, *Army Special Operations Forces.*
b. US Air Force Doctrine Document 3-05, *Special Operations.*
c. USSOCOM Publication 1, *Special Operations.*
d. USSOCOM Publication 3-11, *Multiservice Tactics, Techniques, and Procedures for Special Operations Forces in Nuclear, Biological, and Chemical Environments.*
e. USSOCOM Document 525-7, *Special Operations Liaison Element (SOLE).*

APPENDIX B

Administrative Instructions

1. User Comments

Users in the field are highly encouraged to submit comments on this publication to: Commander, United States Joint Forces Command, Joint Warfighting Center Code JW100, 116 Lake View Parkway, Suffolk, VA 23435-2697. These comments should address content (accuracy, usefulness, consistency, and organization), writing, and appearance.

2. Authorship

The lead agent for this publication is the United States Special Operations Command. The Joint Staff doctrine sponsor for this publication is the Director for Operations (J-3).

3. Supersession

This publication supersedes JP 3-05, 17 December 2003, *Doctrine for Joint Special Operations*.

4. Change Recommendations

a. Recommendations for urgent changes to this publication should be submitted:

TO: CDRUSSOCOM MACDILL AFB FL//SOOP-PJ-D//
INFO: JOINT STAFF WASHINGTON DC//J7-JDETD//
            CDRUSJFCOM SUFFOLK VA//JW100//

Routine changes should be submitted to the Director for Joint Force Development (J-7), JDETD, 7000 Joint Staff Pentagon, Washington, DC 20318-7000, with info copies to the USJFCOM JWFC.

b. When a Joint Staff directorate submits a proposal to the Chairman of the Joint Chiefs of Staff that would change source document information reflected in this publication, that directorate will include a proposed change to this publication as an enclosure to its proposal. The Military Services and other organizations are requested to notify the Director, J-7, Joint Staff, when changes to source documents reflected inthis publication are initiated.

c. Record of Changes:

CHANGE NUMBER	COPY NUMBER	DATE OF CHANGE	DATE ENTERED	POSTED BY	REMARKS

5. Distribution of Publications

Local reproduction is authorized and access to unclassified publications is unrestricted. However, access to and reproduction authorization for classified JPs must be in accordance with DOD 5200.1-R, *Information Security Program*.

6. Distribution of Electronic Publications

a. Joint Staff J-7 will not print copies of JPs for distribution. Electronic versions are available on the Joint Doctrine, Education, and Training Electronic Information Systemat https://jdeis.js.mil (NIPRNET), and https://jdeis.js.smil.mil (SIPRNET) and on the JEL at http://www.dtic.mil/doctrine (NIPRNET).

b. Only approved JPs and joint test publications are releasable outside the combatant commands, Services, and Joint Staff. Release of any classified JP to foreign governments or foreign nationals must be requested through the local embassy (Defense Attaché Office) to DIA, Defense Foreign Liaison/IE-3, 200 MacDill Blvd., Bolling AFB, Washington, DC 20340-5100.

Special Operations 113

c. CD-ROM. Upon request of a joint doctrine development communitymember, the Joint Staff/J-7 will produce and deliver one CD-ROM with current JPs.

GLOSSARY

Part I—Abbreviations and Acronyms

AE	aeromedical evacuation
AFSOC	Air Force special operations component
AFSOD	Air Force special operations detachment
AFSOE	Air Force special operations element
AFSOF	Air Force special operations forces
AOI	area of interest
AOR	area of responsibility
ARSOC	Army special operations component
ARSOF	Army special operations forces
ASOC	air support operations center
C2	command and control
CA	civil affairs
CAISE	civil authority information support element
CAO	civil affairs operations
CAP	crisis action planning
CASEVAC	casualty evacuation
CBRN	chemical, biological, radiological, and nuclear
CbT	combating terrorism
CCDR	combatant commander
CDRJSOTF	commander, joint special operations task force
CDRTSOC	commander, theater special operations command
CDRUSSOCOM	Commander, United States Special Operations Command
CF	conventional forces
CJCSI	Chairman of the Joint Chiefs of Staff instruction
CJTF	commander, joint task force
CMO	civil-military operations
CNA	computer network attack
CND	computer network defense
CNE	computer network exploitation
CNO	computer network operations
COA	course of action
COCOM	combatant command (command authority)
COIN	counterinsurgency
COM	chief of mission
CP	counterproliferation
CT	counterterrorism
DA	direct action

DIOCC	Defense Intelligence Operations Coordination Center
DJTFAC	deployable joint task force augmentation cell
DOD	Department of Defense
DOS	Department of State
DSPD	defense support to public diplomacy
EW	electronic warfare
FID	foreign internal defense
FSF	foreign security forces
GCC	geographic combatant commander
GCTN	global combating terrorism network
GEOINT	geospatial intelligence
HN	host nation
HNS	host-nation support
HQ	headquarters
IA	information assurance
IDAD	internal defense and development
IGO	intergovernmental organization
IO	information operations
ISB	intermediate staging base
IW	irregular warfare
JAOC	joint air operations center
JCMOTF	joint civil-military operations task force
JFACC	joint force air component commander
JFC	joint force commander
JFSOC	joint force special operations component
JFSOCC	joint force special operations component commander
JIOC	joint intelligence operations center
JIPOE	joint intelligence preparation of the operational environment
JMISC	Joint Military Information Support Command
JMISOTF	joint military information support operations task force
JP	joint publication
JSOA	joint special operations area
JSOAC	joint special operations air component
JSOACC	joint special operations air component commander
JSOTF	joint special operations task force
JTAC	joint terminal attack controller
JTF	joint task force
LNO	liaison officer
MARSOC	Marine Corps special operations command
MARSOF	Marine Corps special operations forces
METOC	meteorological and oceanographic
MILDEC	military deception
MISO	military information support operations
MNF	multinational force
NAVSOC	Navy special operations component
NAVSOF	Navy special operations forces

NGO	nongovernmental organization
NICC	National Intelligence Coordination Center
NSWTF	naval special warfare task force
NSWTG	naval special warfare task group
OGA	other government agency
OPCON	operational control
OPSEC	operations security
PA	public affairs
PN	partner nation
RC	Reserve Component
RFI	request for information
ROE	rules of engagement
SecDef	Secretary of Defense
SF	special forces
SFA	security force assistance
SO	special operations
SOA	special operations aviation (Army)
SOC	special operations component
SOCCE	special operations command and control element
SOF	special operations forces
SOJTF	special operations joint task force
SOLE	special operations liaison element
SO-peculiar	special operations-peculiar
SOTF	special operations task force
SR	special reconnaissance
SSR	security sector reform
TA	target audience
TACON	tactical control
TACP	tactical air control party
TSOC	theater special operations command
USC	United States Code
USG	United States Government
USJFCOM	United States Joint Forces Command
USSOCOM	United States Special Operations Command
USSTRATCOM	United States Strategic Command
UW	unconventional warfare
WMD	weapons of mass destruction

Part II—Terms and Definitions

aeromedical evacuation. The movement of patients under medical supervision to and between medical treatment facilities by air transportation. Also called **AE.** (JP 1-02. SOURCE: JP 4-02)

Air Force special operations base. None. (Approved for removal from JP 1-02.)

Air Force special operations detachment. A squadron-size headquarters that could be a composite organization composed of different Air Force special operations assets, normally subordinate to an Air Force special operations component. Also called **AFSOD.** (Approved for incorporation into JP 1-02.)

Air Force special operations element. None. (Approved for removal from JP 1-02.)

Air Force special operations forces. Those Active and Reserve Component Air Force forces designated by the Secretary of Defense that are specifically organized, trained, and equipped to conduct and support special operations. Also called **AFSOF.** (JP 1-02. SOURCE: JP 3-05)

architecture. None. (Approved for removal from JP 1-02.)

area assessment. None. (Approved for removal from JP 1-02.)

area oriented. None. (Approved for removal from JP 1-02.)

armed reconnaissance. None. (Approved for removal from JP 1-02.)

Army special operations forces. Those Active and Reserve Component Army forces designated by the Secretary of Defense that are specifically organized, trained, and equipped to conduct and support special operations. Also called **ARSOF.** (JP 1-02. SOURCE: JP 3-05)

beach landing site. None. (Approved for removal from JP 1-02.)

blocking position. None. (Approved for removal from JP 1-02.)

bridgehead. None. (Approved for removal from JP 1-02.)

campaign plan. A joint operation plan for a series of related major operations aimed at achieving strategic or operational objectives within a given time and space. (JP 1-02. SOURCE: JP 5-0)

casualty evacuation. The unregulated movement of casualties that can include movement both to and between medical treatment facilities. Also called **CASEVAC.** (JP 1-02. SOURCE: JP 4-02)

center of gravity. The source of power that provides moral or physical strength, freedom of action, or will to act. Also called **COG.** (JP 1-02. SOURCE: JP 3-0)

civil administration. An administration established by a foreign government in (1) friendly territory, under an agreement with the government of the area concerned, to exercise certain authority normally the function of the local government; or (2) hostile territory, occupied by United States forces, where a foreign government exercises executive, legislative, and judicial authority until an indigenous civil government can be established. Also called **CA**. (JP 1-02. SOURCE: JP 3-05)

civil affairs. Designated Active and Reserve Component forces and units organized, trained, and equipped specifically to conduct civil affairs operations and to support civil-military operations. Also called **CA**. (JP 1-02. SOURCE: JP 3-57)

civil affairs operations. Those military operations conducted by civil affairs forces that (1) enhance the relationship between military forces and civil authorities in localities where military forces are present; (2) require coordination with other interagency organizations, intergovernmental organizations, nongovernmental organizations, indigenous populations and institutions, and the private sector; and (3) involve application of functional specialty skills that normally are the responsibility of civil government to enhance the conduct of civil-military operations. Also called **CAO**. (JP 1-02. SOURCE: JP 3-57)

civil-military operations. The activities of a commander that establish, maintain, influence, or exploit relations between military forces, governmental and nongovernmental civilian organizations and authorities, and the civilian populace in a friendly, neutral, or hostile operational area in order to facilitate military operations, to consolidate and achieve operational US objectives. Civil-military operations may include performance by military forces of activities and functions normally the responsibility of the local, regional, or national government. These activities may occur prior to, during, or subsequent to other military actions. They may also occur, if directed, in the absence of other military operations. Civil-military operations may be performed by designated civil affairs, by other military forces, or by a combination of civil affairs and other forces. Also called **CMO**. (JP 1-02. SOURCE: JP 3-57)

combatant command (command authority). Nontransferable command authority established by Title 10 ("Armed Forces"), United States Code, Section 164, exercised only by commanders of unified or specified combatant commands unless otherwise directed by the President or the Secretary of Defense. Combatant command (command authority) cannot be delegated and is the authority of a combatant commander to perform those functions of command over assigned forces involving organizing and employing commands and forces, assigning tasks, designating objectives, and giving authoritative direction over all aspects of military operations, joint training, and logistics necessary to accomplish the missions assigned to the command. Combatant command (command authority) should be exercised through the commanders of subordinate organizations. Normally this authority is exercised through subordinate joint force commanders and Service and/or functional component commanders. Combatant command (command authority) provides full authority to organize and employ commands and forces as the combatant commander considers necessary to accomplish assigned missions. Operational control is inherent in combatant command (command authority). Also called **COCOM**. (JP 1-02. SOURCE: JP 1)

combating terrorism. Actions, including antiterrorism and counterterrorism, taken to oppose terrorism throughout the entire threat spectrum. Also called **CbT**. (JP 1-02. SOURCE: JP 3-26)

combined joint special operations task force. None. (Approved for removal from JP 1-02.)

conventional forces. 1. Those forces capable of conducting operations using nonnuclear weapons. 2. Those forces other than designated special operations forces. Also called **CF.** (JP 1-02. SOURCE: JP 3-05)

counterinsurgency. Comprehensive civilian and military efforts taken to defeat an insurgency and to address any core grievances. Also called **COIN.** (JP 1-02. SOURCE: JP 3-24)

counterterrorism. Actions taken directly against terrorist networks and indirectly to influence and render global and regional environments inhospitable to terrorist networks. Also called **CT.** (JP 1-02. SOURCE: JP 3-26)

covert operation. An operation that is so planned and executed as to conceal the identity of or permit plausible denial by the sponsor. (Approved for incorporation into JP 1-02.)

cutout. None. (Approved for removal from JP 1-02.)

deception. Those measures designed to mislead the enemy by manipulation, distortion, or falsification of evidence to induce the enemy to react in a manner prejudicial to the enemy's interests. (JP 1-02. SOURCE: JP 3-13.4)

denied area. An area under enemy or unfriendly control in which friendly forces cannot expect to operate successfully within existing operational constraints and force capabilities. (JP 1-02. SOURCE: JP 3-05)

direct action. Short-duration strikes and other small-scale offensive actions conducted as a special operation in hostile, denied, or diplomatically sensitive environments and which employ specialized military capabilities to seize, destroy, capture, exploit, recover, or damage designated targets. Also called **DA.** (Approved for incorporation into JP 1-02.)

foreign internal defense. Participation by civilian and military agencies of a government in any of the action programs taken by another government or other designated organization to free and protect its society from subversion, lawlessness, insurgency, terrorism, and other threats to its security. Also called **FID.** (JP 1-02. SOURCE: JP 3-22)

functional component command. A command normally, but not necessarily, composed of forces of two or more Military Departments which may be established across the range of military operations to perform particular operational missions that may be of short duration or may extend over a period of time. (JP 1-02. SOURCE: JP 1)

guerrilla. None. (Approved for removal from JP 1-02.)

Special Operations

guerrilla force. A group of irregular, predominantly indigenous personnel organized along military lines to conduct military and paramilitary operations in enemy-held, hostile, or denied territory. (JP 1-02. SOURCE: JP 3-05)

in extremis. None. (Approved for removal from JP 1-02.)

insurgency. The organized use of subversion and violence by a group or movement that seeks to overthrow or force change of a governing authority. Insurgency can also refer to the group itself. (JP 1-02. SOURCE: JP 3-24)

intelligence preparation of the battlespace. The analytical methodologies employed by the Services or joint force component commands to reduce uncertainties concerning the enemy, environment, time, and terrain. Intelligence preparation of the battlespace supports the individual operations of the joint force component commands. Also called **IPB.** (JP 1-02. SOURCE: JP 2-01.3)

internal defense and development. The full range of measures taken by a nation to promote its growth and to protect itself from subversion, lawlessness, insurgency, terrorism, and other threats to its security. Also called **IDAD.** (JP 1-02. SOURCE: JP 3-22)

irregular forces. Armed individuals or groups who are not members of the regular armed forces, police, or other internal security forces. (JP 1-02. SOURCE: JP 3-24)

joint combined exchange training. A program conducted overseas to fulfill US forces training requirements and at the same time exchange the sharing of skills between US forces and host nation counterparts. Also called **JCET.** (Approved for incorporation into JP 1-02.)

joint force air component commander. The commander within a unified command, subordinate unified command, or joint task force responsible to the establishing commander for making recommendations on the proper employment of assigned, attached, and/or made available for tasking air forces; planning and coordinating air operations; or accomplishing such operational missions as may be assigned. The joint force air component commander is given the authority necessary to accomplish missions and tasks assigned by the establishing commander. Also called **JFACC.** (JP 1-02. SOURCE: JP 3-0)

joint force commander. A general term applied to a combatant commander, subunified commander, or joint task force commander authorized to exercise combatant command (command authority) or operational control over a joint force. Also called **JFC.** (JP 1-02. SOURCE: JP 1)

joint force special operations component commander. The commander within a unified command, subordinate unified command, or joint task force responsible to the establishing commander for making recommendations on the proper employment of assigned, attached, and/or made available for tasking special operations forces and assets; planning and coordinating special operations; or accomplishing such operational missions as may be assigned. The joint force special operations component commander is given the authority necessary to accomplish missions and tasks assigned by the establishing commander. Also called **JFSOCC.** (JP 1-02. SOURCE: JP 3-0)

joint servicing. That function performed by a jointly staffed and financed activity in support of two or more Services. (Approved for incorporation into JP 1-02.)

joint special operations air component commander. The commander within a joint force special operations command responsible for planning and executing joint special operations air activities. Also called **JSOACC.** (JP 1-02. SOURCE: JP 3-05)

joint special operations area. An area of land, sea, and airspace assigned by a joint force commander to the commander of a joint special operations force to conduct special operations activities. It may be limited in size to accommodate a discrete direct action mission or may be extensive enough to allow a continuing broad range of unconventional warfare operations. Also called **JSOA.** (JP 1-02. SOURCE: JP 3-0)

joint special operations task force. A joint task force composed of special operations units from more than one Service, formed to carry out a specific special operation or prosecute special operations in support of a theater campaign or other operations. Also called **JSOTF.** (Approved for incorporation into JP 1-02.)

Marine Corps special operations forces. Those Active Component Marine Corps forces designated by the Secretary of Defense that are specifically organized, trained, and equipped to conduct and support special operations. Also called **MARSOF.** (JP 1-02. SOURCE: JP 3-05.1)

multinational force. A force composed of military elements of nations who have formed an alliance or coalition for some specific purpose. Also called **MNF.** (JP 1-02. SOURCE: JP 1)

multinational operations. A collective term to describe military actions conducted by forces of two or more nations, usually undertaken within the structure of a coalition or alliance. (JP 1-02. SOURCE: JP 3-16)

multinational warfare. None. (Approved for removal from JP 1-02.)

national security. A collective term encompassing both national defense and foreign relations of the United States. Specifically, the condition provided by: a. a military or defense advantage over any foreign nation or group of nations; b. a favorable foreign relations position; or c. a defense posture capable of successfully resisting hostile or destructive action from within or without, overt or covert. (Approved for incorporation into JP 1-02 with JP 1 as the source JP.)

naval mobile environmental team. None. (Approved for removal from JP 1-02.)

Special Operations 121

naval special warfare. A naval warfare specialty that conducts special operations with an emphasis on maritime, coastal, and riverine environments using small, flexible, mobile units operating under, on, and from the sea. Also called **NSW.** (Approved for incorporation into JP 1-02.)

naval special warfare special operations component. None. (Approved for removal from JP 1-02.)

noncombatant evacuation operations. Operations directed by the Department of State or other appropriate authority, in conjunction with the Department of Defense, whereby noncombatants are evacuated from foreign countries when their lives are endangered by war, civil unrest, or natural disaster to safe havens as designated by the Department of State. Also called **NEOs.** (JP 1-02. SOURCE: JP 3-68)

nongovernmental organization. A private, self-governing, not-for-profit organization dedicated to alleviating human suffering; and/or promoting education, health care, economic development, environmental protection, human rights, and conflict resolution: and/or encouraging the establishment of democratic institutions and civil society. Also called **NGO.** (JP 1-02. SOURCE: JP 3-08)

operational control. Command authority that may be exercised by commanders at any echelon at or below the level of combatant command. Operational control is inherent in combatant command (command authority) and may be delegated within the command. Operational control is the authority to perform those functions of command over subordinate forces involving organizing and employing commands and forces, assigning tasks, designating objectives, and giving authoritative direction necessary to accomplish the mission. Operational control includes authoritative direction over all aspects of military operations and joint training necessary to accomplish missions assigned to the command. Operational control should be exercised through the commanders of subordinate organizations. Normally this authority is exercised through subordinate joint force commanders and Service and/or functional component commanders. Operational control normally provides full authority to organize commands and forces and to employ those forces as the commander in operational control considers necessary to accomplish assigned missions; it does not, in and of itself, include authoritative direction for logistics or matters of administration, discipline, internal organization, or unit training. Also called **OPCON.** (JP 1-02. SOURCE: JP 1)

operational environment. A composite of the conditions, circumstances, and influences that affect the employment of capabilities and bear on the decisions of the commander. Also called **OE.** (JP 1-02. SOURCE: JP 3-0)

operations security. A process of identifying critical information and subsequently analyzing friendly actions attendant to military operations and other activities to: a. identify those actions that can be observed by adversary intelligence systems; b. determine indicators that adversary intelligence systems might obtain that could be interpreted or pieced together to derive critical information in time to be useful to adversaries; and c. select and execute

122 Joint Publication 3-05

measures that eliminate or reduce to an acceptable level the vulnerabilities of friendly actions to adversary exploitation. Also called **OPSEC.** (JP 1-02. SOURCE: JP 3-13.3)

overt operation. An operation conducted openly, without concealment. (JP 1-02. SOURCE: JP 2-01.2)

paramilitary forces. Forces or groups distinct from the regular armed forces of any country, but resembling them in organization, equipment, training, or mission. (JP 1-02. SOURCE: JP 3-24)

personnel recovery. The sum of military, diplomatic, and civil efforts to prepare for and execute the recovery and reintegration of isolated personnel. Also called **PR.** (JP 1-02. SOURCE: JP 3-50)

preparation of the environment. An umbrella term for operations and activities conducted by selectively trained special operations forces to develop an environment for potential future special operations. Also called **PE.** (Approved for inclusion in JP 1-02.)

Rangers. Rapidly deployable airborne light infantry organized and trained to conduct highly complex joint direct action operations in coordination with or in support of other special operations units of all Services. (Approved for incorporation into JP 1-02.)

resistance movement. An organized effort by some portion of the civil population of a country to resist the legally established government or an occupying power and to disrupt civil order and stability. (Approved for incorporation into JP 1-02 with JP 3-05 as the source JP.)

SEAL delivery vehicle team. United States Navy forces organized, trained, and equipped to conduct special operations with SEAL delivery vehicles, dry deck shelters, and other submersible platforms. (Approved for inclusion in JP 1-02.)

SEAL team. United States Navy forces organized, trained, and equipped to conduct special operations with an emphasis on maritime, coastal, and riverine environments. (Approved for replacement of "sea-air-land team" and its definition in JP 1-02.)

security force assistance. The Department of Defense activities that contribute to unified action by the United States Government to support the development of the capacity and capability of foreign security forces and their supporting institutions. Also called **SFA.** (JP 1-02. SOURCE: JP 3-22)

special activities. None. (Approved for removal from JP 1-02.)

special boat team. United States Navy forces organized, trained, and equipped to conduct or support special operations with combatant craft and other small craft. Also called **SBT.** (Approved for incorporation into JP 1-02.)

Special Operations 123

special forces. US Army forces organized, trained, and equipped to conduct special operations with an emphasis on unconventional warfare capabilities. Also called **SF.** (JP 1-02. SOURCE: JP 3-05)

special forces group. The largest Army combat element for special operations consisting of command and control, special forces battalions, and a support battalion capable of long duration missions. Also called **SFG.** (Approved for incorporation into JP 1-02.)

special forces operations base. None. (Approved for removal from JP 1-02.)

special operations. Operations requiring unique modes of employment, tactical techniques, equipment and training often conducted in hostile, denied, or politically sensitive environments and characterized by one or more of the following: time sensitive, clandestine, low visibility, conducted with and/or through indigenous forces, requiring regional expertise, and/or a high degree of risk. Also called **SO.** (Approved for incorporation into JP 1-02.)

special operations command. A subordinate unified or other joint command established by a joint force commander to plan, coordinate, conduct and support joint special operations within the joint force commander's assigned operational area. Also called **SOC.** (JP 1-02. SOURCE: JP 3-05)

special operations command and control element. A special operations element that is the focal point for the synchronization of special operations forces activities with conventional forces activities. Also called **SOCCE.** (Approved for incorporation into JP 1-02.)

special operations forces. Those Active and Reserve Component forces of the Military Services designated by the Secretary of Defense and specifically organized, trained, and equipped to conduct and support special operations. Also called **SOF.** (JP 1-02. SOURCE: JP 3-05.1)

special operations liaison element. A special operations liaison team provided by the joint force special operations component commander to the joint force air component commander (if designated), or appropriate Service component air command and control organization, to coordinate, deconflict, and integrate special operations air, surface, and subsurface operations with conventional air operations. Also called **SOLE.** (JP 1-02. SOURCE: JP 3-05)

special operations-peculiar. Equipment, material, supplies, and services required for special operations missions for which there is no Service-common requirement. Also called **SO-peculiar.** (Approved for incorporation into JP 1-02.)

special operations weather team. A task organized team of Air Force personnel organized, trained, and equipped to collect critical environmental information from data sparse areas. Also called **SOWT.** (Approved for replacement of "special operations weather team/tactical element" and its definition in JP 1-02.)

124   Joint Publication 3-05

special reconnaissance. Reconnaissance and surveillance actions conducted as a special operation in hostile, denied, or politically sensitive environments to collect or verify information of strategic or operational significance, employing military capabilities not normally found in conventional forces. Also called **SR.** (Approved for incorporation into JP 1-02.)

special tactics. None. (Approved for removal from JP 1-02.)

special tactics team. An Air Force task-organized element of special tactics that may include combat control, pararescue, tactical air control party, and special operations weather personnel. Also called **STT.** (Approved for incorporation into JP 1-02.)

subordinate unified command. A command established by commanders of unified commands, when so authorized by the Secretary of Defense through the Chairman of the Joint Chiefs of Staff, to conduct operations on a continuing basis in accordance with the criteria set forth for unified commands. A subordinate unified command may be established on an area or functional basis. Commanders of subordinate unified commands have functions and responsibilities similar to those of the commanders of unified commands and exercise operational control of assigned commands and forces within the assigned operational area. Also called subunified command. (JP 1-02. SOURCE: JP 1)

subversion. Actions designed to undermine the military, economic, psychological, or political strength or morale of a governing authority. (JP 1-02. SOURCE: JP 3-24)

tactical control. Command authority over assigned or attached forces or commands, or military capability or forces made available for tasking, that is limited to the detailed direction and control of movements or maneuvers within the operational area necessary to accomplish missions or tasks assigned. Tactical control is inherent in operational control. Tactical control may be delegated to, and exercised at any level at or below the level of combatant command. Tactical control provides sufficient authority for controlling and directing the application of force or tactical use of combat support assets within the assigned mission or task. Also called **TACON.** (JP 1-02. SOURCE: JP 1)

task-organizing. None. (Approved for removal from JP 1-02.)

terrorism. The unlawful use of violence or threat of violence to instill fear and coerce governments or societies. Terrorism is often motivated by religious, political, or other ideological beliefs and committed in the pursuit of goals that are usually political. (JP 1-02. SOURCE: JP 3-07.2)

theater special operations command. A subordinate unified command established by a combatant commander to plan, coordinate, conduct, and support joint special operations. Also called **TSOC.** (Approved for incorporation into JP 1-02.)

Special Operations

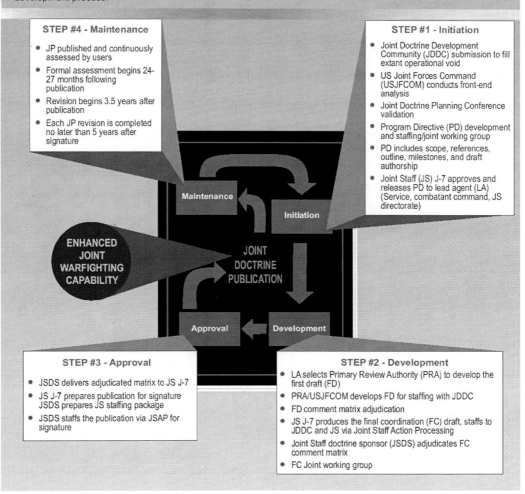

unconventional warfare. Activities conducted to enable a resistance movement or insurgency to coerce, disrupt, or overthrow a government or occupying power by operating through or with an underground, auxiliary, and guerrilla force in a denied area. Also called **UW.** (Approved for incorporation into JP 1-02.)

weapons of mass destruction. Chemical, biological, radiological, or nuclear weapons capable of a high order of destruction or causing mass casualties and exclude the means of transporting or propelling the weapon where such means is a separable and divisible part from the weapon. Also called **WMD.** (JP 1-02. SOURCE: JP 3-40)

In: U.S. Special Operations Forces
Editor: Michael E. Harris and Roger L. Cook

ISBN: 978-1-61470-507-9
© 2011 Nova Science Publishers, Inc.

Chapter 4

POSTURE STATEMENT OF ADMIRAL ERIC T. OLSON, USN COMMANDER, UNITED STATES SPECIAL OPERATIONS COMMAND, BEFORE THE 112TH CONGRESS, HOUSE ARMED SERVICES COMMITTEE

Eric T. Olson

Mr. Chairman and distinguished members of the Committee, thank you for this opportunity to provide an update on the United States Special Operations Command (USSOCOM) . Our Special Operations Forces give us much cause for great pride and it is my deep privilege to represent them to you, and especially to do so for the fourth time as their commander.

My intent today is to describe the current status, activities and requirements of Special Operations Forces. I'll begin by briefly describing USSOCOM and its assigned Special Operations Forces.

As many of you know, USSOCOM is a creation of Congress, legislated into being in 1986. A relatively small number of Army, Navy and Air Forces units designated as Special Operations Forces were assigned to USSOCOM, with Marine Corps forces joining the Command just over five years ago.

Before the establishment of USSOCOM, the Nation's Special Operations Forces had generally not been treated as a top priority. They now thrive under the focused attention of a single headquarters and a dedicated budget. In the 24 years since USSOCOM was established, Special Operations Forces have repeatedly proven their value, often under extraordinarily demanding conditions.

In many ways, USSOCOM is a microcosm of the Department of Defense, with ground, air and maritime components, a global presence, and authorities and responsibilities that mirror the Military Departments, Military Services and Defense Agencies. We take pride in the diversity of our people and our mission.

One of our headquarter' s functions is to synchronize Department of Defense planning against terrorists and their networks globally. This is complex work that connects us across DoD and into other U.S. Government departments and other nations' military forces. The effects of this are manifested in a series of planning documents that guide specific actions by the Services and Combatant Commands.

Primarily, USSOCOM organizes, trains and equips Special Operations Forces and provides those forces to the Geographic Combatant Commanders under whose operational control they serve. The Command also develops special operations strategy, doctrine and procedures for SOF employment and develops and procures specialized equipment for the force.

Our key subordinate commands are U.S. Army Special Operations Command, Naval Special Warfare Command, U.S. Air Force Special Operations Command, Marine Corps Forces Special Operations Command and Joint Special Operations Command. Within these commands are the legendary Special Forces or Green Berets, SEALs, Air Commandos, Rangers, Night Stalker helicopter crews, and the modern version of yesterday's Marine Raiders. Our force also includes the active duty practitioners of Civil Affairs Operations and Military Information Support Operations, and all of the instructors, logisticians, administrators, analysts, planners, communicators, doctrine writers and other specialists who are key to our ability to meet our Nation's needs. Most are active duty military, but we depend heavily on our Guard and Reserve units and the government civilians and contractors who perform duties that don't require a uniformed service member.

We now total close to 60,000 people, about a third of whom are career members of Special Operations Forces, meaning those who have been selected, trained and qualified to earn the Military Occupational Specialty or skill code identifier of a SOF operator.

The activities of the force are as varied as its character. From high-risk, high-intensity counterterrorist raids; to meticulous intelligence analysis; to providing first response during a natural disaster; to launching from submerged submarines; to training and accompanying foreign counterparts; to working with local leaders to determine what will bring value to their village; to providing supporting precision fires to fighting troops from orbiting aircraft – SOF personnel are in vital roles, in key places, performing essential tasks.

Our presence is generally small and agile, inherently joint and persistent. Our formations normally include an array of attached capabilities that are necessary to optimize the force – including female Cultural Support Teams, Tactical Air Controllers, Military Working Dogs, interpreters, maintenance and repair personnel, Explosive Ordnance Disposal technicians and others. SOF rarely dominate an area with their mass, so they must work with indigenous forces and the local civilian population to accomplish their missions. This is often complicated, demanding and high-risk.

Each of the Geographic Combatant Commanders who will appear before you is well served by the Special Operations Forces that are deployed to his region, although the balance is heavily weighted towards U.S. Central Command. In fact, about 85 percent of deployed SOF are directly engaged in Operations NEW DAWN and ENDURING FREEDOM. I will defer to the regional commanders to highlight the contributions of Special Operations Forces in their theaters. I will just say here that, although the precision counterterrorism missions certainly receive the most attention, SOF are conducting a wide range of activities in dozens of countries around the world on any given day – at the request of the host government, with the approval of the U.S. Ambassador and under the operational control of the U.S. Geographic Combatant Commander.

To support these forces and activities, USSOCOM invested in many specialized programs and equipment. As the commander responsible for the preparation and readiness of

SOF, I focus on developing and sustaining operational skills and capabilities, training and maintaining the quality of the force, caring for its families, and ensuring that our people have the right equipment in sufficient quantity. I also carefully monitor global military and political trends in my role as the senior advisor on the employment of SOF.

Among USSOCOM's most important functions is the management of Major Force Program–11 (MFP-11). MFP-11 is provided to the Commander of USSOCOM to address requirements that are "SOFpeculiar" in nature, and it is the essential fuel that enables Special Operations Forces to meet the Nation's needs. It provides for the conduct of advanced and unique training, the timely and flexible fielding of equipment, and the capability to rapidly and effectively project our force. In Fiscal Year 2012, the request for MFP-11 funds totals $10.5 billion in baseline and Overseas Contingency Operations (OCO) funding. This is an increase of 7 percent over the FY11 request, and every dollar is necessary to meet the ever-increasing demands placed on our Special Operations Forces.

At the forefront of budget discussions is the acknowledgment that many of the current expenditures funded by OCO are, in fact, part of USSOCOM' s baseline requirement in the "new normal." This was highlighted by the Department last year when a commitment was made to eventually move funding required to execute Overseas Contingency Operations into the baseline as part of the SECDEF's initiative to "rebalance" the force. However, USSOCOM will continue to rely on OCO funding over the next few years as the phased transfer to the base budget occurs. For example, in the FY 2012 budget submission thirty-four percent of the total MFP-11 request is OCO funding. For some higher intensity SOF elements, the OCO percentage is greater than 75 percent. USSOCOM will carefully prioritize and manage the OCO to base transition. Overall, we are in a fiscally satisfactory condition, but the force requires continued support. The President's Budget Request for FY12, if approved, is an essential step towards meeting the growing demand on our force by providing USSOCOM the resources required to sustain critical programs and initiatives. Now, I would like to highlight some of these key efforts.

PROGRAMS

USSOCOM continues to expand and recapitalize its rotary and fixed wing aviation fleets. This year we began modification of the last of the originally planned 61 MH-47G helicopters, while starting procurement of eight additional MH-47Gs. We are also fielding the first of 72 planned MH-60M helicopters as part of our recapitalization of MH-60 K/L platforms. The tilt-rotor CV-22, having demonstrated its capabilities on multiple deployments, must remain on plan to ensure enhanced future mobility capabilities for SOF. USSOCOM's MC-130Ws, rapidly modified with a Precision Strike Package utilizing SOF' s Joint Acquisition Task Force, are providing armed overwatch and mobility to deployed SOF as an interim augmentation to our Vietnam-era AC-130 gunship fleet. We are on a path to ultimately recapitalize the gunships with AC-130J models. The MC-130J program is on track to replace our aging MC-130Es and MC-130Ps. Our Non-Standard Aviation Program is delivering a variety of smaller aircraft to provide intra-theater airlift capacity and we continue to grow our aviation foreign training capability in support of the Geographic Combatant Commanders' engagement plans.

USSOCOM is also modernizing its maritime mobility systems. We will award competitive prototype contracts later this year for Combatant Craft – Medium (CCM) as replacements for the Naval Special Warfare Rigid Hull Inflatable Boat (RHIB). We have realigned resources from the Advanced SEAL Delivery System (ASDS) and the Joint Multi-Mission Submersible (JMMS) to fund the development of a family of Dry Submersibles as part of our undersea mobility strategy. These will be launched from surface ships or Dry Deck Shelter-equipped submarines. As part of this modernization program, we will explore expansive and flexible approaches that are supportive of the Secretary of Defense's intent to streamline acquisition processes and accelerate delivery times.

Special Operations Forces continue to rely on a wide range of ground mobility vehicles, often leveraging Service and Department investments. Modified to meet the wide variety of SOF mission sets and provide enhanced crew protection, vehicles such as the MRAP have been essential to SOF teams operating in dispersed and rugged terrain throughout the USCENTCOM Area Of Responsibility. These vehicles, as well as our other ground mobility systems, will remain relevant well into the future as we synchronize our long-term sustainment strategy with the Services.

We continue to invest in airborne manned and unmanned Intelligence, Surveillance and Reconnaissance (ISR) programs, relying heavily on the Services to expand capabilities and capacity that benefit DoD across the board. USSOCOM is moving toward a relatively small number of manned and unmanned ISR systems; essential Processing, Exploitation, and Dissemination (PED) capabilities; and supporting communications architectures.

One of the most noteworthy improvements within special operations over the last few years has been the growth of advanced communications and networking capabilities through our expeditionary SOF Information Enterprise (SIE). As our portion of the Department's Global Information Grid, the SIE provides network independence while maintaining connectivity into the global interface, and links Special Operations Forces across the globe into a common network. This connectivity shortens the decision cycle for SOF operators worldwide and allows more rapid information sharing. The research and rapid development of these types of technologies is an inherent strength of special operations.

USSOCOM, inherently joint in all it does, is in a unique position to leverage and apply Service and Department Science and Technology (S&T) efforts to rapidly field new technologies on the battlefield. USSOCOM's "Rapid Exploitation of Innovative Technologies for SOF" (REITS) program, enables innovative new capabilities to be developed and inserted quickly into the battlefield - advanced "talk and jam" capabilities for SOF vehicles; mobile repair and maintenance "shops in a box"; to solar panel energy technology that supports SOF in remote locations. USSOCOM also seeks to expand its biomedical research and development activities. To date, USSOCOM has pushed "state of the art" combat medicine with modest resources through the Tactical Combat Casualty Care program. However, we also have great need to explore innovative methods of treating our wounded members so that they may be reintegrated and returned to duty as rapidly as possible.

As a force that operates from the tropics to the Arctic regions, from under water to high elevations, and from peaceful areas to violent combat zones, Special Operations Forces serve as an ideal "control group" for Service R&D investments that can result in significant benefits across DoD.

USSOCOM' s development of the Joint Acquisition Task Force (JATF) concept enabled accelerated acquisition and fielding of urgent SOF capabilities. First demonstrated on the

MC-130W Dragon Spear program, USSOCOM expanded use of the JATF concept to address many emerging requirements of SOF warfighters. Innovative approaches such as the JATF, coupled with a professionally trained and certified SOF acquisition corps that stays in close and frequent contact with the operators, continue to ensure that USSOCOM remains as a vanguard of rapid acquisition within DoD.

USSOCOM's acquisition planning, collaboration, and continuing dialogue with the Services continues to improve as we become more efficiently effective while rapidly moving capabilities to the warfighter. USSOCOM, in conjunction with USD AT&L, initiated a series of Acquisition Summits with the Military Department Acquisition Executives to minimize programmatic disconnects and to better align requirements, co-sponsorship opportunities, funding efficiencies, and contracting actions among MFP-11 programs and Service-related/dependent programs. These periodic meetings offer a level of transparency among all our accounts that enables us to seek common solutions for Service-wide requirements and to better invest in SOF-peculiar modifications or special capabilities. This forum identified several opportunities, which if supported by Congress, would enable more efficient execution of SOF unique acquisitions.

USSOCOM is making a significant investment in Military Construction (MILCON) to address shortfalls resulting from fielding new capabilities, a growing force structure and aging infrastructure that was inherited without a future recapitalization budget. To address the shortfall, the Command's 2012 budget submission is based on a MILCON roadmap that identifies over 300 prioritized requirements valued at more than $5 billion between 2012 and 2025. Specifically, our FY12 budget submission includes 33 of these projects, valued at $631M across eight states and representing 9 percent of the Command's projected base budget request – a near record level. This investment demonstrates a commitment to addressing our critical infrastructure needs. To continue this effort, the Command's new Strategic Planning and Programming Guidance raised the MILCON funding minimum from 4 to 6 percent to support this priority in future budgets.

A Congressional action that enhanced the effectiveness of our force is our Section 1208 authority. This authority to reallocate limited MFP-11 funds remains a key tool used by widely dispersed SOF to leverage indigenous forces in support of counterterrorism operations. USSOCOM is appreciative of the increase to $45 million provided by Congress in the FY11 National Defense Authorization Act, as it provides us the ability to support ongoing operations with a measure of flexibility should a contingency arise. Continuation of Section 1208 authority provides enhanced effectiveness to our force both strategically and tactically.

INITIATIVES

Our primary challenge is the need to carefully manage the growth of Special Operations Forces, even in these periods of high demand, in order to ensure the continued quality the nation expects. I have stated in my last three posture hearings that SOF's organic manpower growth should be in the range of 3-5 percent per year. That is the pace we have sustained to great effect over the past several years and our FY12 budget submission continues this pace. But 3-5 percent growth within USSOCOM will not answer the increasing demand for our force unless it is matched by the Military Services' commitment to attach supporting and enabling forces at a commensurate rate. SOF units must include a limited amount of these enabling forces to ensure rapid response to emerging requirements, but we were designed and intended to rely on the Services to meet most of our combat support and combat service support requirements. In order to establish a predictable demand signal for these Service-provided capabilities, USSOCOM is proposing changes to the way we build, train, deploy and sustain a fully enabled force.

To better build the SOF team, we are developing a force generation system that engages the existing Service systems. In 2011, USSOCOM will strive to create a SOF Force Generation system that will be synchronized with the Services, matching their capabilities with our Special Operations core units in time to provide fully optimized force packages to the Geographic Combatant Commanders. For elements organic to SOF, such as our Civil Affairs and Military Information Support Operations, we will expand their capacities to meet the increasing demand for their capabilities.

Another challenge we face is how to effectively prepare and train the force to achieve enhanced interoperability with the General Purpose Forces (GPF). Currently in the USCENTCOM AOR, SOF is executing the counterterrorist strike mission and theVillage Stability Operations mission; two of the primary lines of operation underpinning the Afghanistan strategy. SOF's key role in both is creating opportunities for enhanced interoperability with the GPF such as the deployment of the 1ST Battalion, 16TH Infantry, now assigned to the Combined Joint Special Operations Task Force – Afghanistan (CJSOTF-A); a sea change in SOF-GPF relations. Currently, we are developing initiatives that will increase inter-operational effectiveness prior to the deployment phase of the operation.

In 2011, we will continue to review and coordinate changes to Service personnel policies to further incentivize language pay for key languages such as Pashto, Dari and Arabic. We will work to develop courses of action that allow SOF reliable and predictable access to Service resources such as training ranges for our ground and aviation elements. The shortage of readily available, local ranges currently hampers SOF's ability to meet deployment training timelines and causes our operators to "travel to train," further increasing their already excessive time away from home.

Understanding the operational context of the environments in which we operate is a hallmark of SOF. Developing this knowledge and experience within our force, and understanding the value of "micro-regional" expertise allows SOF to conduct its activities with more predictable outcomes. While immersion opportunities enhance our regional sophistication, our training can never develop the level of nuanced understanding possessed by indigenous populations. To gain this high level of cultural knowledge, USSOCOM will continue to strongly support DoD's Military Accessions Vital to the National Interest (MAVNI) and the Army's Intermediate and Advanced Language Programs (IALP) to recruit and access the requisite expertise provided by native speakers. Additionally, our attached female Cultural Support Teams (CSTs) allow us to reach key elements of the population in some environments which was not previously possible. This concept of attaching females to SOF units is effective and long overdue; we are urging the Services to recognize the capabilities of CSTs as essential military skills.

Finally, our efforts to become more innovative include studying the best practices of other organizations. For example, we are inspired by the ability of the World War II's Office of Strategic Services to rapidly recruit specialized talent, develop and acquire new technologies and conduct effective global operations within the period of its relatively brief existence.

To further our engagement with our international allies and partners, and within the U.S. interagency community, USSOCOM will continue to expand the Special Operations Liaison Officer (SOLO) and Special Operations Support Team (SOST) programs. Both of these outreach efforts provide SOF experts to support and enhance their host organizations while serving as SOF liaisons. Our priority is to assign SOLO officers wherever a foreign partner has, or is planning to establish, a USSOCOM-like headquarters.

Joint operations and special operations are two growing trends in many of our partner nation military forces. One manifestation is the recent establishment of the NATO SOF Headquarters. In accordance with the 2010 National Defense Authorization Act, the Secretary of Defense designated USSOCOM as the lead component for this Headquarters – a role we will embrace and expand in an effort to advise and assist an interoperable network of global SOF.

Importantly, we remain committed to caring for our service members and their families. I am concerned about the effects of nine years of focus on combat operations on the well-being of our extended special operations community. To support the wounded and injured and their caregivers, the Command remains committed to our Special Operations Care Coalition and the Tactical Human Optimization, Rapid Rehabilitation and Reconditioning (THOR3) Program. Both programs are focused on long term care, rehabilitation and reintegration of our warriors. In an additional effort to be predictive and preventive, I established a "Pressure on the Force" Task Force to survey and analyze the effects of repetitive combat deployments over nearly a decade. Necessarily relying on soft data, collective experiences and commanders' instincts, it will try to determine what initiatives might help ease the strain and contribute to long term retention and force stability. I expect to receive the recommendations from this team within 90 days.

In conclusion, I will reinforce what I believe are the top challenges to the Command. As the Chairman of the Joint Chiefs of Staff recently stated, "...the first forces in are typically Special Forces. And the last ones out are going to be Special Forces." As we expect to remain the force of first choice for many military operations, USSOCOM must:

1. Carefully and deliberately meet the ever-increasing demand for Special Operations Forces.
2. Improve and expand our tactical and operational level skills, equipment and systems.
3. Preserve our proposed budget levels and authorities.
4. Find better structures and processes to obtain Service- provided capabilities.
5. Continue to improve our acquisition speed and agility.
6. Better understand the people and conditions in the places we go, whether to assist or fight.
7. As our most solemn duty, look after the health and well-being of this magnificent force from whom we ask so much.

Today's Special Operations Forces are the most capable, best prepared SOF in history. Their ingenuity, perseverance, spirit and skill continue to inspire and amaze. In significant ways, they have emerged from the shadows to make visible and dramatic impacts of great magnitude. It is my honor to have served within SOF for the last 37 years and to represent this extraordinary force today before this committee.

As always, our success is only possible because of your continued support and advocacy. Your approval of the President's Budget Request will help ensure our continued ability to address some of our Nation's most daunting security challenges.

CHAPTER SOURCES

Chapter 1 - This is an edited, reformatted and augmented version of a Congressional Research Service publication, RS21048, dated March 28, 2011.

Chapter 2 - This is an edited, reformatted and augmented version of a United States Special Operation Command Fact Book publication.

Chapter 3 - This is an edited, reformatted and augmented version of a Special Operations Joint Publication, JP 3-05.

Chapter 4 - This is an edited, reformatted and augmented version of a Posture statement of Admiral Eric T. Olson before the 112th Congress, House Armed Services Committee, dated March 3, 2011.

INDEX

A

access, 2, 9, 47, 59, 66, 70, 96, 100, 109, 112, 132
acquisitions, 131
adaptability, 22, 61
administrative support, 45
administrators, 128
adverse effects, 68, 109
adverse weather, 4, 25
advocacy, 134
Afghanistan, 5, 7, 15, 72, 132
Africa, 4, 23, 50
age, 4
agencies, 25, 36, 43, 48, 60, 71, 74, 76, 80, 94, 96, 102, 105, 118
agility, 82, 133
ambassadors, 27
armed conflict, 58, 62, 72, 103
armed forces, 29, 74, 119, 122
assault, 10, 36, 38, 68
assessment, 25, 37, 67, 69, 70, 75, 116
assets, vii, viii, 1, 4, 10, 47, 53, 55, 61, 66, 67, 69, 70, 79, 82, 85, 88, 89, 92, 96, 97, 99, 100, 105, 108, 116, 119, 124
authorities, 3, 16, 21, 66, 78, 79, 80, 94, 109, 117, 127, 133
authority, vii, 1, 8, 16, 17, 54, 55, 65, 78, 79, 81, 83, 84, 85, 86, 91, 92, 94, 98, 100, 105, 113, 116, 117, 119, 121, 124, 131
avoidance, 34
awareness, 36, 56, 59, 63, 70, 75, 76, 89, 97, 109

B

Bahrain, 29
base, 29, 37, 38, 99, 100, 114, 115, 123, 129, 131
behaviors, 26

Belgium, 6
benefits, 8, 67, 72, 130
Boat, 5, 8, 29, 30, 31, 32, 130

C

campaigns, 61, 62, 63, 71, 72, 75, 76, 78
candidates, 9, 23
CAP, 97, 113
caregivers, 133
chain of command, 55, 73, 81, 83, 89, 94
challenges, 68, 90, 94, 133, 134
chemical, 67, 69, 70, 113
Chief of Staff, 4
City, 30
civil society, 121
classes, 22, 37
collaboration, 74, 131
collateral, 24, 68, 109
collateral damage, 109
combined effect, 77
commercial, 79, 101, 105
communication, 61, 72, 94, 95, 101, 103, 107, 108
communication skills, 94
community, 2, 17, 22, 23, 36, 65, 96, 133
compatibility, 101
complement, 61, 65, 68, 69, 77
composition, 93, 96, 107
computer, 77, 104, 108, 113
conference, 10
conflict, 20, 23, 62, 64, 72, 90, 121
conflict resolution, 121
confrontation, 64
connectivity, 101, 130
consensus, 94
contingency, 4, 5, 21, 26, 27, 29, 46, 49, 57, 58, 62, 63, 72, 89, 97, 98, 99, 100, 101, 103, 131
control group, 130

138 Index

cooperation, 18, 50, 62, 63, 75, 96
coordination, 20, 29, 39, 55, 56, 57, 58, 59, 60, 63, 71, 73, 74, 78, 79, 81, 82, 86, 91, 92, 94, 95, 98, 99, 101, 103, 104, 105, 109, 117, 122
cost, 6
counterterrorism, vii, 1, 6, 8, 9, 49, 54, 60, 113, 117, 118, 128, 131
crises, 78
critical infrastructure, 131
culture, 61
curriculum, 23
customers, 90
cyberspace, 64, 107, 108
cycles, 91

D

decentralization, 91
decision makers, 63, 76, 77
deficiencies, 67
Delta, 6
denial, 118
Department of Defense, vii, 1, 2, 8, 10, 11, 22, 37, 48, 65, 110, 114, 121, 122, 127
deployments, vii, 1, 4, 7, 18, 25, 37, 46, 50, 90, 129, 133
destruction, 70, 71, 126
detachment, 113, 116
detection, 109
deterrence, 59, 62, 63, 105
developed nations, 101
developing nations, 23
development assistance, 76
diplomacy, 109, 114
diplomatic efforts, 75
direct action, 3, 20, 23, 25, 29, 34, 36, 46, 54, 61, 113, 118, 120, 122
directives, 7, 58, 99, 103
disaster, 17, 27
disclosure, 95
discrimination, 76
disposition, 61
distribution, 98, 112
diversity, 49, 60, 127
domestic laws, 103
downsizing, 9

E

economic development, 121
education, 16, 20, 22, 36, 37, 47, 65, 74, 78, 121
electromagnetic, 108

embassy, 73, 94, 112
emergency, 25, 39, 100, 103
emergency management, 103
employees, 43, 57, 98
employment, viii, 20, 50, 53, 55, 57, 59, 61, 65, 66, 72, 76, 78, 79, 82, 83, 85, 91, 95, 105, 107, 119, 121, 123, 128, 129
endurance, 45
enemies, 6, 64
energy, 108, 130
England, 4, 36
environment, 5, 25, 46, 55, 57, 62, 64, 67, 68, 71, 74, 75, 76, 77, 78, 80, 81, 83, 90, 95, 97, 98, 107, 108, 114, 119, 121, 122
environmental conditions, 25, 106
environmental effects, 106
environmental protection, 121
environmental regulations, 2, 10
equipment, vii, 2, 6, 7, 8, 16, 38, 43, 46, 48, 56, 57, 65, 66, 67, 74, 89, 95, 98, 99, 101, 104, 105, 122, 123, 128, 129, 133
ethnic groups, 74
Europe, 4, 6, 49
evacuation, 58, 68, 96, 100, 109, 113, 115, 116, 121
evidence, 103, 118
execution, 48, 49, 50, 56, 57, 59, 63, 67, 70, 77, 79, 89, 90, 91, 92, 93, 95, 99, 103, 104, 106, 107, 108, 131
executive orders, 58, 103
exercise, 5, 10, 29, 47, 81, 84, 85, 116, 119, 124
expenditures, 16, 129
expertise, 5, 22, 49, 56, 58, 78, 81, 89, 90, 104, 123, 132
exploitation, 108, 113, 122
extraction, 32, 33, 34, 38
extremists, 70

F

families, 2, 9, 129, 133
fear, 26, 70, 124
federal agency, 58, 78, 79, 103
federal law, 58, 103
financial, 73
fires, 128
flexibility, 45, 46, 79, 81, 82, 91, 101, 131
flight, 4, 41
flooding, 34, 35
foreign language, 3, 27, 95
foreign nationals, 112
foreign policy, 74
forward presence, 4, 35

Index   139

freedom, 59, 107, 116
friction, 90, 109
funding, 8, 17, 129, 131
funds, vii, 1, 8, 129, 131

G

Galaxy, 32
Germany, 30, 49
global communications, 59, 105
global economy, 60
gravity, 76, 116
growth, 7, 9, 119, 130, 131
guidance, 36, 58, 60, 63, 68, 81, 102
guidelines, 60, 66, 78, 103

H

harmony, 94
Hawaii, 30, 49
hazards, 38, 69
health, 58, 100, 101, 103, 104, 121, 133
health care, 100, 121
height, 40, 41, 42, 43
history, vii, 133
hospitalization, 100
host, 17, 27, 32, 35, 39, 46, 58, 60, 114, 119, 128, 133
hostilities, 50
House, v, 7, 10, 11, 64, 127
human, 24, 27, 107, 121
human right, 24, 121
human rights, 24, 121

I

ideal, 130
identification, 55, 63, 74, 81, 83, 98, 101, 104
identity, 118
image, 58, 103
imagery, 59, 103, 105
images, 103
immersion, 132
immigrants, 60
improvements, 130
independence, 130
individuals, 8, 61, 71, 74, 78, 105, 119
information sharing, 71, 130
information technology, 108
infrastructure, 27, 71, 99, 103, 108, 131
injuries, 33
insertion, 32, 34

institutions, 22, 79, 96, 109, 117, 121
insurgency, 17, 72, 73, 75, 76, 118, 119, 126
Insurgency, 119
integration, 37, 50, 54, 56, 62, 63, 65, 70, 71, 74, 79, 81, 90, 91, 98
integrity, 22, 82, 103
intelligence, viii, 9, 16, 23, 35, 38, 39, 45, 46, 47, 48, 53, 57, 59, 61, 67, 69, 72, 73, 74, 76, 91, 92, 95, 96, 97, 103, 104, 105, 106, 108, 109, 114, 119, 121, 128
intelligence gathering, 38
interface, 4, 8, 35, 96, 101, 130
interference, 21, 109
interoperability, 6, 16, 48, 63, 77, 82, 90, 91, 92, 109, 132
intervention, 75
investment, 8, 131
investments, 130
ions, 63
Iran, vii, 17
Iraq, 1, 4, 7, 9, 11, 15
isolation, 61, 108
issues, vii, 1, 24, 58, 92, 103, 105

J

Japan, 4, 36

K

kill, 25
Korea, 14, 49

L

language skills, 43, 75
languages, 132
law enforcement, 73
lead, 3, 9, 29, 47, 63, 71, 74, 78, 79, 81, 89, 98, 111, 133
leadership, 2, 9, 76, 78, 90, 108
legislation, 18
light, 3, 7, 20, 122
logistics, 28, 29, 45, 47, 67, 95, 98, 99, 100, 117, 121

M

magnitude, 134
majority, 4, 61, 73, 91, 99
man, 28

management, 20, 27, 67, 80, 96, 98, 129
manipulation, 118
manpower, vii, 1, 5, 7, 43, 76, 131
Marine Corps, vii, viii, 2, 3, 5, 9, 10, 17, 18, 43, 45, 46, 47, 56, 59, 65, 86, 88, 104, 114, 120, 127, 128
masking, 69
mass, 4, 23, 35, 70, 126, 128
mass media, 4
materials, 99
matter, iv, 23, 105
media, 48, 78, 109
mediation, 63
medical, 3, 5, 21, 36, 39, 58, 66, 67, 100, 109, 115, 116
medical care, 100
medicine, 130
mentoring, 64
messages, 78, 79, 103
mid-career, 8
miscommunication, vii, 17
misconceptions, 90
models, 8, 129
modernization, 130
modifications, 131
morale, 77, 124
multiplier, 81

N

National Defense Authorization Act, 8, 131, 133
national interests, 73
national security, 16, 78, 120
NATO, 6, 10, 49, 133
natural disaster, 78, 103, 121, 128
natural disasters, 78, 103
networking, 130
neutral, 107, 109, 117
NGOs, 65, 71, 79, 80, 104
nodes, 61, 63, 108
nuclear weapons, 70, 126
nucleus, 46, 87

O

Obama, 7
officials, 74
operating system, 61
Operation Enduring Freedom, 5, 50
Operation Iraqi Freedom, 50
opportunities, 83, 90, 91, 131, 132
organ, 21, 37, 43, 128

organize, 23, 28, 39, 46, 62, 117, 121
outreach, 48, 133
oversight, 1, 2, 9, 20, 29, 78

P

Pacific, 4, 23, 49
parallel, 95
participants, 89, 94
peace, 21, 24, 49
peacekeeping, 24
Pentagon, 7, 11, 112
permit, 32, 33, 91, 118
perseverance, 133
personal relations, 57, 94
personal relationship, 57, 94
persuasion, 94
platform, 37, 39
police, 23, 74, 119
policy, 23, 70, 71, 78, 79, 80, 99
politics, 56, 89
popular support, 76
population, 27, 49, 64, 74, 76, 109, 122, 128, 132
poverty, 60
predictability, 8
preparation, iv, 57, 68, 72, 95, 106, 109, 114, 119, 122, 128
preparedness, 16, 23
preservation, 100
president, 18, 39
President, 7, 16, 17, 18, 63, 82, 83, 117, 129, 134
prevention, 27, 55, 79, 82, 94
primary function, 39
principles, 56, 60, 82, 90
professional careers, 23
professional development, 36
professional growth, 22
professionalism, 38
profit, 121
project, 129
proliferation, 20, 23, 70
proportionality, 76
protection, 33, 39, 40, 58, 100, 103, 104, 130
prototype, 8, 130
public affairs, 58, 79, 115
publishing, 23

Q

qualifications, 29, 38

Index

R

R&D investments, 130
radio, 35, 79
real estate, 98
reasoning, 78
recommendations, iv, 3, 5, 7, 55, 83, 85, 119, 133
recovery, 25, 27, 29, 35, 36, 39, 68, 69, 104, 122
recruiting, 37
reform, 17, 74, 115
regeneration, 66
rehabilitation, 133
relevance, 66
reliability, 20
relief, 78
repair, 128, 130
reproduction, 112
resistance, 72, 73, 122, 126
resolution, 72
resource allocation, 3
resources, 3, 5, 18, 21, 27, 54, 66, 67, 71, 80, 92, 97, 101, 108, 129, 130, 132
response, 50, 62, 63, 73, 78, 89, 96, 97, 103, 128, 132
responsiveness, 20, 91
restructuring, 74
rhythm, 56, 90
risk, viii, 10, 21, 24, 46, 53, 61, 66, 67, 68, 72, 77, 79, 97, 103, 123, 128
risks, 54, 67
root, 27
rules, 58, 94, 115

S

sabotage, 68
safe haven, 121
safe havens, 121
safety, 105
sanctions, 63
saving lives, 39
school, 20, 37, 47
science, 48
scope, 57, 61, 62, 68, 71, 84, 93, 95, 97
scripts, 10
Secretary of Defense, 1, 2, 9, 18, 43, 48, 54, 63, 102, 115, 116, 117, 120, 123, 124, 130, 133
secure communication, 92
security, 5, 17, 24, 29, 38, 46, 48, 50, 54, 55, 57, 61, 62, 63, 72, 73, 74, 75, 76, 81, 83, 96, 97, 98, 101, 104, 105, 108, 109, 114, 115, 118, 119, 121, 122, 134

security assistance, 24, 29
security forces, 17, 74, 75, 76, 114, 119, 122
seizure, 36, 68
self-sufficiency, 61
Senate, 7, 11, 17
sensitivity, 58, 69, 102
sensors, 70
sequencing, 93
shape, 62, 71, 103, 108
shortage, 132
shortfall, 67, 131
showing, 8
signs, 8
skills training, 36, 37, 46, 80, 89
social network, 56, 89
society, 118
solution, 2, 63
Somalia, 15
sovereign state, 72
sovereignty, 74
span of control, 82
specialists, 48, 78, 128
stability, 27, 46, 62, 72, 73, 74, 81, 122, 133
stabilization, 21
staff members, 23
stakeholders, 27
standardization, 6, 48, 101
state, vii, 1, 7, 20, 31, 43, 50, 64, 90, 101, 130
states, 62, 64, 74, 77, 131
stress, 2, 9
structure, vii, 1, 5, 9, 10, 18, 27, 47, 54, 55, 57, 65, 75, 81, 82, 83, 88, 90, 91, 95, 98, 100, 120, 131
submarines, 5, 8, 31, 32, 128, 130
supervision, 63, 100, 115
supporting institutions, 74, 122
surgical intervention, 100
surveillance, 35, 42, 43, 57, 59, 69, 70, 95, 104, 105, 124
sustainability, 74
synchronization, 55, 82, 91, 123
synchronize, 18, 56, 58, 62, 67, 77, 91, 92, 104, 127, 130
synergistic effect, 71

T

tactics, 6, 11, 16, 29, 36, 38, 39, 48, 65, 68, 70, 88, 96, 124
talent, 132
Taliban, 72
tanks, 40

target, 26, 39, 43, 67, 68, 69, 77, 92, 96, 107, 108, 115
team members, 80
teams, 3, 7, 11, 23, 27, 29, 43, 45, 46, 54, 58, 59, 65, 66, 70, 79, 80, 90, 92, 96, 100, 102, 105, 109, 130
techniques, viii, 6, 10, 22, 53, 61, 68, 69, 123
technologies, 130, 133
technology, 29, 70, 78, 103, 130
telephone, 34
tempo, 56, 57, 90, 92, 93, 98
tensions, 62
territory, vii, 2, 36, 39, 57, 69, 71, 98, 104, 116, 119
terrorism, 8, 16, 23, 29, 70, 71, 72, 73, 75, 76, 113, 114, 117, 118, 119, 124
terrorist organization, 70, 71
terrorists, 6, 29, 70, 71, 127
threats, 5, 17, 29, 46, 58, 70, 73, 75, 100, 103, 118, 119
training, vii, 2, 3, 4, 5, 6, 8, 9, 16, 17, 20, 22, 23, 25, 29, 34, 37, 39, 45, 47, 48, 49, 54, 61, 64, 65, 66, 74, 75, 76, 78, 90, 94, 104, 107, 109, 117, 119, 121, 122, 123, 128, 129, 132
training programs, 22
transcripts, 11
transformation, 28
transmission, 58, 103
transparency, 131
transport, 10, 32, 45, 100, 101
transportation, 115
trauma, 39
treatment, 100, 115, 116

U

U.S. policy, 21
U.S. Treasury, 3

United, v, 10, 11, 13, 16, 18, 27, 39, 53, 54, 55, 61, 63, 64, 65, 70, 71, 72, 74, 77, 79, 82, 110, 111, 113, 115, 116, 117, 120, 122, 127
United States, v, 10, 11, 13, 16, 18, 27, 39, 53, 54, 55, 61, 63, 64, 65, 70, 71, 72, 74, 77, 79, 82, 110, 111, 113, 115, 116, 117, 120, 122, 127

V

variables, 73
vehicles, 31, 122, 130
Vietnam, 14, 129
violence, 46, 60, 74, 119, 124
violent extremist, 27, 64, 70, 71
vision, 58, 103
visualization, 97, 103
vulnerability, 67

W

war, 21, 23, 26, 50, 60, 62, 63, 68, 71, 77, 81, 121
Washington, 11, 112
water, 31, 34, 130
weapons, 17, 33, 36, 37, 47, 54, 65, 70, 97, 105, 108, 115, 118, 126
weapons of mass destruction (WMD), 54, 70, 71, 115, 126
wear, 8
well-being, 133
windows, 59, 106
withdrawal, 68
World War I, 132
worldwide, vii, 1, 5, 6, 20, 21, 24, 25, 28, 29, 43, 46, 47, 65, 66, 82, 101, 130